CONCILIUM

CONCILIUM   2015/3

GLOBALIZATION AND THE CHURCH OF THE POOR

Edited by

Daniel Franklin Pilario, Lisa Sowle Cahill, Maria Clara Bingemer & Sarojini Nadar

SCM Press · London

Published in 2015 by SCM Press, 3rd Floor, Invicta House,
108–114 Golden Lane, London EC1Y 0TG.

SCM Press is an imprint of Hymns Ancient & Modern Ltd (a registered charity)
13A Hellesdon Park Road, Norwich NR6 5DR, UK

www.concilium.in

ISBN 978-0-334-03134-5

Printed in the UK by
Ashford Press, Hampshire

Contents

Part Three: Theological Forum

Editorial
Globalization and the Church of the Poor

'The poor ... the poor are at the centre of the Gospel, are at heart of the Gospel, if we take away the poor from the Gospel we can't understand the whole message of Jesus Christ,' emphasized Pope Francis in his spontaneous faltering English at a Mass for the clergy and religious at the Manila Cathedral on 16 January 2015. As if to prove his point, the next day he decided to fly to the island of Leyte – the so-called 'Ground Zero' of the typhoon Haiyan – despite a raging storm. And on the makeshift stage, battered by strong winds and dripping with rain, he celebrated the Eucharist in front of more than 200,000 people already drenched in the previous night's stormy weather, as they had prepared to meet him. Despite the thin yellow raincoat, which he wore like the rest of the crowd, he was also wet together with them. Deciding not to read his English homily, he spoke from his heart in Spanish with the help of his translator: '*Permítanme esta confidencia – cuando yo vi desde Roma esta catástrofe, sentí que tenía que estar aquí. Esos días decidí hacer el viaje aquí. Quise venir para estar con ustedes, un poco tarde me dirán, es verdad, pero estoy.*'[1] This dramatic gesture of solidarity warmed the hearts of all who gathered, most of whom were survivors and had lost families and property a little more than a year ago during the strongest typhoon recorded in recent history.

If there is anything that characterizes Pope Francis' pastoral approach, it is these dramatic gestures that concretize solidarity in and with the 'Church of the Poor', among others, his apparently spontaneous choice of the name 'Francis', when Cardinal Hummes of São Paulo reminded him to 'remember the poor'. There was also the unprecedented act of washing the feet of young convicts, including a Muslim woman, in a traditional Holy Thursday ritual in Casal del Marmo as well as his visit to the island of Lampedusa, where a banner read: 'Welcome among the *ultimi!*' (an Italian word meaning 'the furthest and the least'). And the list continues.

7

These daring gestures are also matched with powerful words. Phrases hinting at some decisive social analysis have become popular catchwords much to the disappointment of the economic and political right: economy of exclusion, globalization of indifference, throw-away culture, economy that kills, scandal of poverty, idolatry of money, culture of waste and so on. Condemnations of self-referential attitudes have become media favourites, as they also keep the 'eminences' on their toes: spiritual worldliness, feeling immortal and indispensable, mental and spiritual petrification, existential schizophrenia, sterile pessimism, spiritual desertification, rivalry, gossip and vainglory. And with these words also came some initial decisive action: the restructuring of the Vatican Bank, reform of the Roman curia, decentralization of power etc. Is the so-called 'Pope Francis effect' more style than substance? It will require time to ascertain the answer, as the Pope implements his vision at the practical level. But his vision of the Church is decisively clear and popular: 'I would like to see a Church that is poor and for the poor.' 'I prefer a Church which is bruised, hurting and dirty, because it has been out on the streets, rather than a Church which is unhealthy from being confined and from clinging to its own security.' And his challenge is as direct and simple: 'Go to the peripheries'... 'Go, and make a mess!'

The 'Church of the Poor' discourse is not new; it has a long history. What makes the present Francis revival seemingly novel is the fact that the 'Option for the Poor' has been eclipsed, domesticated and disciplined in the previous decades. The efforts of Cardinal Ratzinger, then the Prefect of the CDF, to censure Gustavo Gutierrez through a letter sent to the Peruvian bishops in 1983 is widely known.[2] Gutierrez was never officially censured, but the Vatican came out with *Libertatis nuntius* a year later, almost echoing the same accusations against some currents of liberation theology. Other liberation theologians suffered the same fate – Leonardo Boff, Pedro Casaldaliga, Tissa Balasuriya and others. As recently as 2006, Jon Sobrino was sent a CDF Notification precisely on his use of the notion of the 'Church of the Poor' in his book *Jesus the Liberator*.[3] One of Sobrino's primary methodological deficiencies, the CDF writes, is 'the affirmation that the "Church of the poor" is the ecclesial "setting" of Christology and offers it its fundamental orientation'.[4] It is because of this starting point that his Christology has been judged deficient. For the CDF, 'it is only the apostolic faith which the Church has transmitted through all generations that constitutes the ecclesial setting of Christology and of theology in general'.[5] But Sobrino's assertion of the 'primacy of the poor' (and the Church of the Poor) is no different from what Pope Francis now proclaims in *Evangelii gaudium*: 'That is why I want a Church that is poor and for the poor. They have much to teach us. Not only do they share in the sensus fidei but in their difficulties they know the suffering of Christ' (*EG* 198). In other words, without neglecting the importance of the apostolic faith, it is the poor's experience of suffering that makes their lives a fundamental location for the Church to know Jesus; it is 'the ecclesial setting of Christology' to use the words of the CDF Notification. What was once 'condemned' now becomes central to magisterial thought, just as Gustavo Gutierrez was already welcomed in the Vatican and the cause of Monsignor Oscar Romero, once side-lined, is now nearing beatification.

The contribution of Paulo Fernando Carneiro de Andrade in this volume traces the 'Church of the Poor' discourse to the historic radio message of John XXIII before Vatican II, the debates within the Vatican Council itself, its Latin American reception, the birth of liberation theology and the crisis it encountered after the pontificate of Paul VI. While some writers triumphantly proclaim the 'retreat of liberation theology'[6] during those moments of crisis, Andrade argues that Pope Francis' discourse is in fact a confirmation and reaffirmation of the Church of the Poor 'in its original sense' that has been present all along – as it was already found in the discussions in Vatican II, the Pact of the Catacombs, Medellín, Puebla, Santo Domingo, Aparecida and subsequent Latin American praxis.

Beyond this original setting, this present issue also attempts to explore 'the joys and hopes, the griefs and anxieties' of men and women, particularly the new faces of the poor in different contexts, in this globalized age. As 'globalization' gains greater currency in the twenty-first century, it is the intention of the articles in this volume to inquire into how this global economic order affects the lives of the poor, the Church communities and the way we do theology. Due to globalization, poverty has expanded into multifaceted spheres – e.g. gender, race, classes, ethnicity, religions and others. But even these new forms have already mutated into newer shapes and dimensions. For instance, widespread migration has changed the demographics, gender and cultural–religious constitution of both sending and host countries, not to mention the unfathomable socio-psychological costs of this phenomenon. The rise of new local elites in developing countries challenges the terrains of the old racial identity politics in post-conflict and neoliberal global contexts. The ever-increasing forms of cultural destruction of indigenous communities and plunder of natural resources driven by profit perpetuate the colonial project at more intense and destructive levels. These new developments necessitate rethinking of our sociological analyses, theological categories and pastoral interventions.

Maryann Cusimano Love, a political scientist, examines globalization and its complex relationship with poverty. Positive assessments of the phenomenon, she asserts, are grounded on GDP-based frameworks which might show some reduction in poverty in some parts of the world like India or China. Further investigation, however, proves this to be problematic. The world's 85 richest people have more wealth than half of the world's population. Even within developed economies, the blessings of global capital have not really 'trickled down'. Globalization intrudes more into weakly governed states. Corporations move freely but workers do not, especially in developing and underdeveloped countries. The author challenges the Catholic Church, itself a global institution, to promote 'institutional pluralism' – a collaborative effort in global governance among state, non-state and pre-state actors as one systemic response that will ultimately 'put people before profits'.

The article of biblical scholars Carlos Mesters and Francisco Orofino recall, in a pastoral and somewhat colloquial style, the great Latin American experience of popular reading of the Bible. Since the 1970s, the Bible has been something that gave impulse to communities in the grassroots struggling for liberation. The spread of the biblical and popular movement helped communities to face the challenges of military dictatorships, which persecuted and tortured the poor and those who struggled for and with them. But new situations in our globalized world pose new methodological issues and challenges to the popular reading of the Bible – among others, the feminist or gender question, the prevalence of fundamentalist interpretations, the longing for spirituality in liberationist readings, the perspectives of indigenous peoples, the demand for a deeper study of the Bible among grassroots communities and the lack of professional advisers. Using metaphors from the Book of Revelation, Mesters and Orofino identify the shift in context from the 'old beast' (i.e. national security state) to the new one (i.e. global neoliberalism). The task is to find appropriate methods of reading the Bible to respond to these new challenges.

From the South African situation, Gerald O. West's article takes 'human dignity' as the theological key with which to understand the political struggle of the poor in the new South Africa. For West, the struggle among South Africa's poor has shifted from a political to a moral one; from achieving revolutionary objectives to demanding fundamental human dignity as being able to enjoy their basic human needs – housing, safety, health care, political representation. While the old colonial racist structure was engaged in systemic exploitation, the new neoliberal capitalist enclave, now composed of the black African elite, wreaks havoc through systemic neglect in their refusal to grant this basic dignity. West challenges socially engaged biblical scholars to bring biblical scholarship to the peripheries – to borrow a phrase from Pope Francis – and together with them, forge a people's theology that retrieves 'the prophetic trajectory of dignity's revolt in the Bible'.

From a totally different context, Etienne Grieu starts his article by asking which forces in today's world have the power to resist the seemingly universal and ubiquitous rule of globalization. Reflecting on his experience in *Diaconia*[7] – a three-year program of the dioceses of France that culminated in a national gathering in Lourdes in May 2013 – Grieu identifies those whose lives are locked in extreme poverty and misery (*ceux qui ne comptent pas*) to lead the Church towards the path of resistance. In these meetings, the floor was given to the poor for them to share their pains and fears, their joys, hopes and proposals for survival. Grieu emphasizes that commitment towards humiliated peoples cannot be seen as struggles that take place only outside of the churches. On the contrary, churches really begin to be meaningful when they accept to be disturbed by and to learn from the poor. It is only by being transformed by this encounter that they can begin to proclaim the gospel.

Jung Mo Sung's article argues that Pope Francis' analysis of global capitalism as 'social exclusion' is a product not only of hard socio-economic analysis or timely cultural assessment but, more appropriately, of a theological critique that strikes at the heart of Christian theology. The Pope's critique of the 'idolatry of money' (*EG* 55) as the new version of the worship of the golden calf (Exod. 32.1–35) was already present in the early intuitions of liberation theology. Liberation theology has long proclaimed that the problem in Latin America is not atheism but idolatry. Its founding moment is located in the spiritual experience of basic ethical indignation against dominant capitalist structures which transform human beings into

11

'non-persons' bereft of dignity and, in an act of total inversion, enthrones money, profit and development as the new gods to be worshipped. Hugo Assmann, Franz Hinkelammert, Gustavo Gutierrez, Pablo Richard and others had already pointed to this idolatrous character of the market. The present challenge, Sung argues, is to continually unmask these false gods which have gone global and affirm the dignity of their victims as the way to live a non-idolatrous faith.

Part Two of this issue attempts to identify and uncover the workings of globalization exemplified in selected issues prevalent in some continents – migration, piracy of natural resources, drug trafficking and unemployment. Beyond abstract numbers and statistics, our authors reveal how these new forms of poverty further dehumanize concrete persons and marginalize real communities. First, Gemma Tulud Cruz exposes the effects of large-scale migration in Asia, especially among unskilled and undocumented workers considered as the underclass among the migrants. Conditions set by the global market and exploitative immigration policies in their host countries force these 'new slaves' to go undocumented, thus consequently making them more vulnerable to unjust working conditions. Second, Ronilso Pacheco discusses the limits of the War on Drugs policy as the main instrument of public policy to solve the problem of production, consumption and drug trafficking in Latin America. This policy does not only fail to eliminate drug-related violence; it is also used as a tool for US geo-political interference on the continent. Third, Peter Kanyandago discusses how the plunder and piracy of natural resources from the Third World can be traced to Europe's self-proclaimed colonial right to 'discover' other lands with appropriate ecclesiastical and political backing – from papal bulls to international law. In these global times, this plunder takes the form not only of looting Africa's resources, but also of dumping their waste on African soil without care for its consequences on humans and the environment. Fourth, Kenneth Himes's article reflects on the severe problem of unemployment in the USA after the 2007 recession. This situation not only gives us a view of the deep suffering among the unemployed in the once robust economies, but also of the growing inequality leading to 'plutocracy' (the rule by rich for the rich) in the First World.

But we find that the above analyses of global poverty at the same time carry with them some narratives of resistance. The poor even as they are victims are also agents of their own transformation. For instance, migrant

12

churches in host countries often not only serve as the much-needed refuge for migrants who seek assistance of all kinds (from counselling to language classes and job openings), but also provide an empowering space for them to find ways to help other migrants in the spirit of accompaniment and community. It is a case of 'the poor helping the poor', of a Church of the Poor for the poor, of the poor being evangelized, but also becoming evangelizers themselves. One finds a parallel case in Latin America where church communities among the poor in otherwise violence-wracked city suburbs are considered by people as places of shelter and resistance, as communities of moral refuge – a different world where violence and weapons do not (and could not) exercise their dominance. And amid the present-day pillage of Africa's natural resources, resistance is not only located in the churches' official statements and advocacy work, but also heard in the critical voices of church people themselves who courageously question the churches' complicity in such plunder. The same challenge is hurled to the churches of developed countries to exercise their prophetic role and establish a consensus of 'work as the right of everyone' in a global capitalist world which only wants to accumulate profit and discard people.

In Part Three, significant recent events merited reflection from sociological and theological viewpoints. First, Denis Kim writes about Pope Francis' trip to Lampedusa on 8 July 2013 – his first official visit outside of Rome. In that border between fortress Europe and Africa, the Pope attacked the 'globalization of indifference' as he challenged countries and peoples to open their hearts (and borders) to migrants in distressful situations. Second, the sociologist of religion José Casanova updates us on the religious situation of Ukraine following the protests in Maidan in February 2014; the historical and political dynamics among different churches and faith traditions and their public role in Ukraine's volatile political situation. Third, Tina Beattie reflects on the Extraordinary Synod on the Family held in Rome in October 2014 and proposes two major challenges which she hopes to be included in the planning for next year's Synod: the full participation of women speaking as women (not as part of couples) and the bridging of the gap between the West and the rest of the world, for example, the difference of position in sexual ethics between African bishops and their more liberal European counterparts.

The editors express their gratitude to Joaõ Vila-Cha, Rosino Gibellini, Diego Irarrazaval, Einardo Bingemer, Felix Wilfred, Thierry-Marie

Editorial

Courau and Solange Lefebvre for their valuable comments, suggestions and assistance.

Daniel Franklin Pilario, Lisa Sowle Cahill,
Maria Clara Bingemer and Sarojini Nadar

Notes

1. Cf. Pope Francis, 'Homily in Tacloban', http://www.rappler.com/specials/pope-francis-ph/81106-full-text-pope-francis-homily-tacloban#English.
2. See also Congregation of the Doctrine of Faith, 'Ten Observations on the Theology of Gustavo Gutiérrez', in *Liberation Theology: A Documentary History* ed. Alfred T. Hennelly, Maryknoll, NY, 1990, pp. 348–50.
3. Jon Sobrino, *Jesucristo liberador: Lectura histórica-teológica de Jesús de Nazaret* Madrid: 1991; ET: *Jesus the Liberator: A Historical-Theological Reading of Jesus of Nazareth*, Maryknoll, NY, 1993.
4. 'Explanatory Note on the Notification of the Works of Father Jon Sobrino, SJ', http://www.vatican.va/roman_curia/congregations/cfaith/documents/rc_con_cfaith_doc_20061126_nota-sobrino_en.html.
5. 'Explanatory Note'.
6. Edward Lynch, 'The Retreat of Liberation Theology', *Homiletic and Pastoral Review* (1994), pp. 12–21.
7. See 'Diaconia, Servons la Fraternité', http://diaconia2013.fr/.

Part One: Globalization and the Church of the Poor

Putting People before Profits: Globalization and Poverty

MARYANN CUSIMANO LOVE

Pope Francis urges us all to put people before profits. This article examines debates about the relationship between globalization and poverty: Is globalization good for the poor, is it fair, and how can we manage globalization consistent with Christian ethics? Globalization has grown wealth for some (India, China), while excluding others (Sub-Saharan Africa, women) and not attending to wealth distribution. Capital flows are protected; people are not. More ethical means of managing globalization requires new institutional pluralism which includes old, pre-state actors. Jesus of Nazareth was an institutional pluralist. We follow in a faster, more tightly connected world.

Pope Francis leverages the media limelight to put the spotlight on the poor, urging us all to address global poverty. Some politicians decry his stance as 'pure liberal Marxism', while others say he is well-intentioned but factually wrong; globalization is decreasing poverty, and the free market is the history's greatest emancipator from poverty.[1] Others openly admire his message. Pope Francis was named 'Person of the Year' by media outlets as diverse as *Time* and *Fortune* magazines and featured on the cover of *Rolling Stone*.

At the heart of the controversy are disputes about the facts, on the relationship between globalization and poverty, on our moral obligations to promote human life and dignity of poor people and of our agency and options in addressing global poverty. This article will examine these debates – is globalization good for the poor; is it fair; and how can we manage globalization to put people before profits, as Francis urges?

Pope Francis is consistent with previous Church teaching in his message of critiques of global capitalism and of our responsibilities to the poor. In *Evangelii gaudium* (The Joy of the Gospel), Pope Francis

17

says 'No to an economy of exclusion', 'No to the new idolatry of money', 'No to a financial system which rules rather than serves' and 'No to the inequality which spawns violence'. When he says 'this economy kills', he is not speaking metaphorically or using rhetorical flourish. He warns us that 'human beings are themselves considered consumer goods to be used and then discarded' and has launched new initiatives to combat modern-day slavery and human trafficking, where people die as part of the global economy.[2]

I Globalization: Problem or Solution to Global Poverty?[3]

What are the facts? Globalization is the fast, interdependent spread of open society, open economy and open technology infrastructures. In combination these three trends amplify, intensify and reinforce each other, so that the whole equals more than the sum of the parts. There are now more democracies and more free market/capitalist economies than ever before in human history and greater access to cheap, decentralized communications and transportation technologies.[4] There are still many non-democratic systems and countries with high levels of state ownership of economies, but the trend lines are moving in the direction of more open systems and have been moving towards greater openness for over a century and a half.

Globalization is not new. For example, the Catholic Church has been a global institution since shortly after its founding. But globalization today differs from previous periods. The speed, reach, intensity, cost and impacts of the current period of globalization are new. Earlier periods of globalization moved missionaries, trade and colonizers far more slowly, with the speed of feet, animals and sailing ships. Now ideas and capital move around the globe instantly, at the touch of a keystroke; people and products cross borders in hours. This makes twenty-first-century globalization quicker, thicker, deeper and cheaper than in previous centuries, bringing benefits as well as costs. The costs, benefits and impacts of globalization are not evenly distributed, but are asymmetrical and unevenly experienced among the world's seven billion people. While globalization is happening, it is not happening equally everywhere. Some societies are highly globalized (Belgium, Ireland, Singapore), while others remain more distant from global economies, technologies and societies (Myanmar/Burma, Burundi, Bhutan).

While deliberate government policies and international laws have facilitated globalization, particularly since the end of the Second World War, the private sector drives the current era of globalization, and many of globalization's impacts are unintended, such as the spread of disease and human traffickers who prey upon the global system.

Is globalization increasing poverty or increasing wealth? It depends on who and where you are in the world and which measurements for wealth and poverty you use. The protagonists of globalization and laissez-faire capitalism rely heavily on two cases and one metric in their arguments that globalization decreases poverty: absolute poverty in India and China has declined when measured by GDP (gross domestic product) per capita. Fewer people in India and China live on less than $1.25 per day, and because India and China are the world's two most populous countries (with more than a billion people in each country), the world has achieved the millennium development goal of reducing the poorest of the poor to over 1.2 billion people. The reduction of the worst poverty and creation of middle classes in these two countries has been an important achievement in promoting human life and dignity. Extrapolating from this data, proponents of globalization argue that income inequality is decreasing among countries, because economic growth in India and China has closed the income gap between those countries and the richest economies. However, fewer people in the worst deprivation has increased the number of poor people still living in deep poverty; over 2.2 billion people live on less than $2 a day. Not all areas have reduced poverty. In Sub-Saharan Africa (SSA), 'there are more than twice as many extremely poor people living in SSA today (414 million) than there were three decades ago (205 million)'.[5] Also, estimates of China's economic performance, provided by the authoritarian Chinese government, are notoriously suspect. The official Chinese government figures underestimate poverty and overestimate Chinese economic growth.

There are problems with defining poverty by GDP per capita. GDP is a very gross measurement. Taking all the wealth of an entire economy and dividing it by all the people in that country masks poverty, averaging away distribution inequalities, acting as if I had a portion of Bill Gates' wealth. While the poor wish they did have access to the bank accounts of the world's richest people, they do not. The world's 85 richest people have more wealth than half the world's population, the poorest 3.5 billion people on earth. GDP figures average away those distribution problems.

Economists have worked hard to produce more accurate measurements of wealth and poverty. Economists now use purchasing power parity (PPP) to determine how much it costs to live in various countries and thus whether people can live on $2 or $1.25 a day.[6] Economists developed the Human Development Index (HDI), which incorporates data on life expectancy, education, literacy as well as income. Last year, the HDI was further refined to include information on inequality (IHDI), thus showing the actual level of development most people in a society have access to, rather than the inflated level of elites.[7] These more accurate measures show that poverty and human development in Sub-Saharan Africa have not been improving during the current period of globalization. But even these more careful attempts to measure poverty and human development use GDP per capita figures, so include the distortion of those figures.

Monetizing poverty and measuring money by GDP per capita tells a story that globalization has increased wealth in some previously poor countries and therefore that all are better off. Even if the private actors at the top of the global economy benefit most, the assumption is that 'a rising tide floats all boats', and a rising GDP will 'trickle down' within societies to help the poor. This narrative emphasizes individual agency; anyone can benefit from new technologies, open economies and increasingly open societies, because globalization allows individuals and societies to trade on their comparative advantages. Because globalization allows more and more people the means to 'pull themselves up by their bootstraps', the remaining poor are thus to blame for their poverty, according to this narrative. By this view, the poor are poor because they have made bad individual choices (to drink, use drugs, not attend school, not work hard, have children out of wedlock), and their personal failings have led to their poverty, not the system of globalization which offers everyone powerful mechanisms to be liberated from poverty. Ireland and India are attractive examples of countries that have been able to leverage their comparative advantages in the global economy to raise wealth. Ireland and India are English-speaking countries with a time zone differential with other major economies, and both have good education systems. They were able to use globalization to benefit from these comparative advantages, as companies in Europe and North America outsourced their IT servicing and administrative processing tasks; the Irish and Indians work while others sleep, thus allowing the global economy to work 24/7 with fewer interruptions. Proponents argue that globalization's free markets freed

India and Ireland from poverty, more globalization will thus reduce poverty for others, and therefore it would be immoral to limit, slow or regulate globalization. They argue that powerful private markets are effectively growing wealth, better than misguided government policies to regulate or manage markets to reduce poverty.

There are some problems with this narrative. Globalization has not spread free markets to all sectors of the economy. Agriculture and labour markets are not free. Trade in agriculture is still highly restricted for many reasons (protectionist agriculture subsidies, concerns about food safety, national security concerns to maintain domestic food production and not rely excessively on unpredictable global markets, domestic politics, to name a few). Workers cannot move freely around the international system in search of the best jobs. Thus countries (and people) whose comparative advantages are in agriculture and cheap labour are highly restricted in their abilities to leverage their talents in the global economy. Capital and high tech goods move very freely around the system; labour and agricultural products do not. Capital flows are protected; people are not. There are many reasons that there are more poor people in Sub-Saharan Africa than there were three decades ago (poor governance, war), but markets have not been free for countries with comparative advantages in agriculture and cheap labour. Globalization excludes farmers and workers from benefiting from global trade the way that capitalists and bankers benefit from global trade. Thus many countries cannot follow the examples of India and Ireland because the global system excludes their comparative advantages. Globalization allows corporations to move freely across borders to find the cheapest labourers for outsourcing, but it does not allow workers to move freely across borders to find the best jobs, and it does not allow workers to unionize to raise their wages.

Economic exclusion occurs in other ways as well. The positive narrative of globalization argues that rising wealth benefits all, but GDP per capita does not measure whether 'trickle down' to the poor occurs, it assumes it. Increasingly economists have been studying questions of poverty and wealth distribution within societies and have found rising income inequality even within developed economies like the USA.[8] This is troubling, because previously it had been thought that income inequality was a temporary phenomenon that was worst in developing countries, but declined over time as capitalist economies matured. New scholarship shows the opposite: rising income inequality even in mature, capitalist economies.[9] Evidence of rising income inequality challenges 'trickle down' assumptions and conflicts with Christian ethics that people come before profits.

II The face of the poor and exclusion: The demographics of global poverty

Poverty is not equally distributed. Women and children suffer most from poverty and economic exclusion. Seventy per cent of the bottom billion, the world's poorest, are women and girls. Seventy per cent of youth not in school are women and girls. Girls are three times more likely to be malnourished. Half of the world's two billion children live in poverty. Women work two-thirds of the world's working hours, but own less than one per cent of the world's property. In many countries, it is illegal for women to own property, have a bank account and inherit property and wealth, which goes to male heirs. If a husband dies, his wife and children are evicted from their homes, as another male relative takes possession. Seventy-five per cent of women are not allowed or able to get bank loans. One billion people are undernourished, and two billion people suffer from micronutrient deficiencies, which lead to poor growth, blindness, increased severity of infections and sometimes death. These trends of economic exclusion hold even in countries where women are allowed to own property and go to school. Two-thirds of those earning the minimum wage in the USA are women and girls. Women hold 75 per cent of the ten lowest-paying jobs, without health benefits: women are 95 per cent of home health aides, 85 per cent of maids and housecleaners, 72 per cent of cashiers and 70 per cent of restaurant workers. Ninety percent of the world's billionaires are men. Distribution problems greatly limit human life and flourishing.

Proponents of globalization argue that these distribution problems have nothing to do with globalization. Patterns of discrimination and exploitation existed prior to the modern period of globalization, therefore are not caused by globalization. Globalization seeks to expand global trade and financial transactions, and thereby grow wealth. It is concerned with easily moving capital and products across borders; it is not concerned with distributing wealth to the poor. As economist Milton Friedman said, the moral responsibility of business is to produce wealth for shareholders, not others.

This is the problem from the point of view of Christian ethics.

Globalization prioritizes easing the global movement of money and stuff, not easing poverty. Catholic social teaching starts from the opposite position, emphasizing the priority of the needs of the poor, the protection of human life and dignity, solidarity with the poor, the dignity of workers, care for creation, participation and subsidiarity. Global mechanisms for speeding goods and capital do not share these priorities.

III The governance problem: Globalizing solidarity in a world of challenged states

Markets need law in order to operate efficiently and justly, but globalization expands global markets to areas where law and governance are weak, leading to greater opportunities for exploitation. The world has a governance problem. We need more of it, at a time when we have less of it. Globalization has created gaps between the problems we face and our abilities to respond. The problems move quickly, but our institutions do not. Problems such as the global financial meltdown, human trafficking and climate change cross borders and require urgent and coordinated action across countries. But governance stops at the borders of our primary institutions, sovereign states. New forms of governance are emerging to fill the gaps, especially in the private sector, sometimes in public-private partnerships, sometimes alone. Civil society combines in transnational networks to change corporate and government behaviour on issues such as debt relief. Non-governmental organizations and private companies provide services previously deemed to be the purview of states – from fighting Ebola to building roads. Civil society and companies develop and hold businesses accountable to corporate social responsibility codes. A private regulatory body governs the internet, to the extent that anyone does. The public sector also attempts to increase capacity and collaboration across borders, by better coordinating state responses, such as the millennium development goals and the post-2015 development agenda to reduce extreme poverty in eight areas, such as increasing universal education and girls' education, and by creating new international institutions (the UN Peacebuilding Commission, the World Trade Organization) and adapting old ones (the World Bank, the UN). Institutional pluralism emerges as these three ways to manage the problems of globalization and reduce poverty are used simultaneously: through state-based responses, through non-state responses and through hybrid, coordinated state and non-state actor partnerships.

Religious actors are part of the mix, because religion is resurgent while states are challenged around the world. Religious actors are not non-state actors, they are pre-state actors, existing millennia before the creation of the modern state system at the Treaty of Westphalia in 1648. Religious actors provide direct services to people in need and sometimes work to strengthen state and international institutions, as when religious actors join with civil society actors to press for better governance through the Publish What You Pay and Extractive Industry Transparency Initiatives, to help the poor by reducing government and business corruption in extractive industries.

All these efforts are still not enough. People are dying, but states cannot save us. Nearly a third of the people on the planet live in the weakest states in the system. These failed and failing states cannot provide drinking water, basic law, order and governance. Their citizens are the most vulnerable, yet these states are the least able to respond to the challenges of globalization.

Governments of countries struggle in a world of institutional pluralism. States are wired to deal with other states; they struggle in how to interact with non-state and pre-state actors.

The Catholic Church, on the other hand, is well positioned to deal with a world of institutional pluralism. The Church is not wed to any single government or market institutional arrangements. It predated sovereign states and modern free markets by millennia, has co-existed with numerous forms of government and market throughout history and today exists around the world under all forms of governance and market arrangements. Ethical considerations such as prioritizing the needs of the poor apply to all organizations. Our challenges are urgent, so we must use all available tools and work through, reform, strengthen, expand and improve many institutions: states, existing and new international institutions, civil society partnerships, more ethically oriented businesses, churches and individuals – all have a role, and no one is off the hook. Pope Francis is not alone in this message. In the encyclical *Caritas in veritate*, Pope Benedict XVI revealed himself to be an institutional pragmatist. Controversy focused on section 67: 'the urgent need of a true world political authority … universally recognized and vested with the effective power to ensure security for all, regard for justice and respect for rights'. Few noted section 41, which urges us 'to promote a dispersed political authority, effective on different levels' and section 57, noting that 'the governance of globalization must be marked by subsidiarity, articulated into several layers and involving different levels that can work together. Globalization certainly requires authority, insofar as it poses the problem of a global common good that needs to be pursued. This authority, however, must be organized in a subsidiary and stratified way.' Catholic teaching calls for effective international institutions, yet also calls for updating and making more ethical and effective all our institutions. The Church neither calls for One World Government nor untrammelled autonomy for markets or states, but for effective global governance. Institutional pluralism carries costs, including overlapping jurisdictions and coordination difficulties. But these institutions already exist, and so can be more quickly reformed to better serve the needs of the world's most vulnerable.

It's an old message. Jesus of Nazareth preached institutional pluralism. He told individuals such as the rich man to sell all he owned and give it to the poor. He told communities, including religious communities, to better care for the poor, and he told his followers to foster and depend upon economic sharing within communities. He told officials to 'render unto Caesar what is Caesar's, and give to God what is God's', much to the disappointment of many Galileans at the time, who urged not paying taxes to the state who they argued overtaxed and mismanaged the money. As a Jew living under foreign occupiers with shifting political boundaries and capacities, Jesus practised what he preached, prioritizing the needs of the most vulnerable among states and markets that did not prioritize the needs of the poor. Today, Pope Francis uses globalization's new transmission and distribution methods to foster these ancient Judeo-Christian ethics, using the methods of globalization to critique the ethical gaps of globalization, urging us all to put people before profits.

Notes

1. Marian Tupo, 'Is the Pope Right About the World? We're living at a far more equal, peaceful, and prosperous time than the pontiff acknowledges', *The Atlantic*, 11 December 2013, http://www.theatlantic.com/international/archive/2013/12/is-the-pope-right-about-the-world/282276/?single_page=true; Sarah Palin, interview on CNN with Jake Tapper, 12 November 2013; Rush Limbaugh, 27 November 2013, http://www.rushlimbaugh.com/daily/2013/11/27/it_s_sad_how_wrong_pope_francis_is_unless_it_s_a_deliberate_mistranslation_by_leftists; Philip Pullella, 'I'm No Marxist, Pope Tells Conservative Critics', *NBC News*, 15 December 2013, http://www.nbcnews.com/news/other/im-no-

marxist-pope-francis-tells-conservative-critics-f2D11748599.
2. Pope Francis, *Evangelii gaudium* 52–60, http://w2.vatican.va/content/francesco/en/
apost_exhortations/documents/papa-francesco_esortazione-ap_20131124_evangelii-
gaudium.html#I.%E2%80%82Some_challenges_of_today%E2%80%99s_world.
3. Maryann Cusimano Love, *Beyond Sovereignty: Issues for a Global Agenda*, New York,
2011.
4. This is not a historical hiccup or accident. Open technologies and increased access
to information helps facilitate democracy movements and undermine state-controlled
economies; more open markets, open societies and open technologies create institutional
mimicry, as societies perceive benefits to organizing in ways that facilitate movement in
global trade and ideas with the majority of other countries. Some try to 'unbundle' these
trends. The Chinese and the Saudis would like profits from open markets while retaining
closed political systems that continue their political power. They would like enough
access to open technologies to produce wealth, but not so much access to information
technologies as to overturn their monopolies on political power and participation and allow
the creation of democratic political systems. Whether or not the Chinese, Saudis and others
will succeed in allowing a little economic freedom while closing off political participation
and access to information technologies and censoring the internet is an experiment being
done on over a billion people. Former President Bill Clinton likens it to 'trying to nail jello
to a wall' and concludes that the attempt is doomed over time. Stay tuned.
5. The World Bank, http://www.worldbank.org/en/topic/poverty/overview.
6. Purchasing power parity tracks how much a basket of needed goods and services (for
example, food, water, housing, clothing) costs in different countries. Using PPP data,
economists have determined higher levels of global poverty particularly in China, which
because of the size of the Chinese economy, impacts the global claims of poverty reduction.
7. In societies where access to education, literacy, long life span and income are more
equally distributed, the previous HDI and current IHDI are nearly identical. Countries
with high levels of inequality, such as the USA and Angola, see their Human Development
Index numbers decrease when inequality is included.
8. Pew Research Center, 'U.S. income inequality, on rise for decades, is now highest since
1928' (December 2013).
9. Thomas Piketty, *Capital in the Twenty-First Century*, Cambridge, MA, 2014.

The 'Option for the Poor' in the Magisterium: Catholic Social Thought from Vatican II to the Aparecida Conference

PAULO FERNANDO CARNEIRO DE ANDRADE

Since the historic radio broadcast of John XXIII, in which he affirmed, one month prior to the opening of the Council, that 'In relation to underdeveloped countries, the Church presents itself as it is and as it wishes to be, that is, as the Church for everyone, and more particularly as the Church of the poor', the question of a Church of the Poor and for the Poor has been greatly developed. In this article, the contribution of the 'Church of the Poor' Group and of Cardinal Lercaro during the Council, the development of the theme in Latin America from Medellín to Aparecida, and the impact of the so-called 'Option for the Poor' by John Paul II will be analysed.

I The historic radio broadcast by John XXIII and the global Context in the 1960s

On 11 September 1962, one month before the beginning of the Second Vatican Council, John XXIII surprised the world and the Church with the following affirmation: 'In relation to underdeveloped countries, the Church presents itself as it is and as it wishes to be, that is as the Church for everyone, and more particularly as the Church of the poor.' That was the moment when, as a result of the Pontiff's words, the theme of the Church of the Poor came centre stage.

Today we are aware that in large measure this radio broadcast reflected the grand plan which had been set out for the Council by Cardinal Suenens, the Primate of Belgium, at the Pope's own request, as an alternative to the schemes prepared by the Curia. The emphasis which Suenens gave, following the wishes of the Pope, was a particularly pastoral one, and the scheme for the Church was elaborated in two parts. The first of these dealt with the Church *ad intra* (which would result in the Dogmatic Constitution *Lumen gentium*), and the other dealt with the Church *ad extra* (which would result in the Pastoral Constitution *Gaudium et spes*). In this plan, in the treatment of the Church *ad extra*, Suenens suggests that the Council ought to concentrate its attention on four main problems, among them the relationship which the Church ought to have with economic society. Suenens explains the necessity for this in the following terms: 'faced with the existence of underdeveloped countries it is necessary that the Church presents itself as the Church for everyone and especially of the poor'.[1]

The theme of poverty and hunger had emerged in a new way in the immediate post-war period. The FAO (Food and Agriculture Organization) had been founded as early as 1945, under the auspices of the UN, with the objective of promoting support for food and nutrition security, especially in poor countries. If prior to this poverty and hunger were widespread problems, present to a greater or lesser degree in every place, now it appeared as a serious problem, localized in some parts of the world, to the extent that it could be said that these regions constituted an underdeveloped 'Third World' (an expression coined by the French geographer Alfred Sauvy in 1952)[2] in the face of the capitalism of the West and the communism of the East. At this time, the 'Third World', as it was conceived, emerged as a new subject for international action. The accelerated process of decolonization which was under way in Asia, the Middle East and Sub-Saharan Africa resulted in the creation of new countries, most of which were characterized by underdevelopment, while being simultaneously the location of independence movements.

The Bandung Conference in April 1955 brought together 29 countries from Asia, the Middle East and Africa and marked the beginning of a coalition of 'Third World' countries, along with the international recognition of a group of new 'Third World' leaders such as Nasser of Egypt, Sukarmo of Indonesia and Chu An-Lai of China. To these names could be added, among others, Kwame Nkrumah (Ghana), Ahmed Sekou Toure (Guinea), Patrice Lubumba (ex-Belgian Congo) and Haile Selasse (Ethiopia). In the meeting held in Belgrade in 1961, the number of participating countries continued to grow and now included Latin America. The principles which were affirmed at this assembly were systematic opposition to imperialism, cooperation between participants in economic affairs and foreign policy, the building of a world based on justice and peace and non-alignment with the two Cold War blocs.

During this period, there was an affirmation both of Pan-Africanism and of Pan-Arabism, as well as of the experience of Arab Socialism. At various times in the 1950s and 1960s, distinctive versions of Arab Socialism were experienced in Egypt, Syria, Algeria, Iraq and South Yemen. In Latin America, the Cuban revolution led to a renewed affirmation of anti-imperial struggle and the rise of movements which found their inspiration in theories of dependency, according to which a process of development in a region can only be launched if it is based on the breaking of the chains of dependency imposed by 'First World' countries which continued to perpetuate the former colonial situation.[3]

In the light of this new reality, questions of the evangelization of the poor and of the presence of the Church in these areas became acute. The Church had already become aware of the distancing that had taken place between itself and the world of the working classes and the poor in Europe since the end of the nineteenth century.[4] This question was becoming more urgent with the rise of secularism and the strengthening of communist parties in Italy and France and the syndical structures that were related to this development. The Church now turned its attention to the 'Third World:'[5] would it also lose the poor who were emerging as new subjects in a world in a process of accelerated transformation?

II The 'Church of the Poor' movement, Cardinal Lecaro and the Second Vatican Council

In this context an informal group which would later come to be known as the 'Church of the Poor' gathered in the Belgian College. Archbishop Melquita Georges Hakim ed Akka-Nararé (Galilee) had inspired Fr Gauthier (a French priest who had been a teacher and director of the Dijon seminary, and who since the mid-1950s had lived in Nazareth, where he had been a worker priest and had formed the religious community 'The Companions of Jesus the Carpenter') to write a preliminary text on the issue.[6] This was circulated among the Council Fathers before the opening of the Council. Identified as being in sympathy with the tenor of this manifesto and responding to an invitation from D. Himmer, the Bishop of

Tournei (Belgium) and D. Hakim, along with a group of 12 bishops, met on 26 October 1962, presided over by Cardinal Gerlier of Lyon (France). Among their number were two Latin Americans whose leadership was very significant, namely Helder Camara (Brazil) and Lanuel Larrain (Chile). In the second meeting, presided over by Patriarch of the Greek Melkite Church in Jerusalem, D. Maximos IV, 50 bishops gathered, among them more bishops from Latin America and North Africa. In order to integrate the group, Cardinal Lercaro of Boulogne was invited, and he was represented by his theological assessor, Fr Dossetti.

In bringing together bishops from various regions, including Europe, the 'Church of the Poor' Group possessed diverse understandings of the question. Some thought of the Church of the Poor as more of a pastoral issue, in the sense of a new pastoral approach to the working classes, while others, such as the Latin Americans, had more of a 'Third-World' perspective, emphasizing that poverty was a result of injustice and stressing the need for the Church to accompany the poor in the process of their liberation struggles. There arose also a tension between an understanding which reduced the issue to pastoral concern, treated more emotively, and another which was doctrinal and political.[7]

Of fundamental importance was the action taken by Cardinal Lercaro, who was to a certain extent independent of the group. On 6 December 1962, in the course of the 35th General Council, Cardinal Lercaro made an extensive speech entitled 'Church and Poverty', which had a major impact. This is a theme he was to take up again and expand upon in a conference called in Beirut on 12 April 1964.[8] Lercaro's position could be summarized as follows:

- The issue of the poor constitutes a mystery which is based on the very mystery of the incarnation. The kenotic process includes the fact that the Word did not simply assume just any flesh (*sarx*), but the flesh of a poor person, and this is no mere coincidence.[9]
- The poor possess a special place in the economy of salvation, as is made clear in the Beatitudes and in the Sermon in the Synagogue at Nazareth, as well as being present in the Messianic prophecies of Isaiah.[10]
- 'Definitively, it is always conformity to Christ in his poverty, his crucifixion and his persecution which saves.'[11]
- 'Concerning the ecclesiological extension of these two characteristics

of Jesus, the Messiah of the poor and the poor Messiah, in as much as the Church is the depositary of the Messianic mission of Jesus, the Church prolongs the mystery of the Kenosis of the Word. The Church cannot be anything other than the Church of the Poor. It gives privilege to its nature as a Church of the Poor in a clearly visible manner in two respects, the first as a church which is before all else the Church of the Poor, with the mission of bringing salvation to the poor and the second as a poor Church,[12]

• For this reason, the question of the Church for the Poor cannot simply be one more theme for the Council to discuss, but has to be the general and overarching theme of the whole Council.

Although it refers to the poor and to poverty at least 63 times,[13] and despite the intensive action of the Church of the Poor Group and of Lercaro, there is only one significant paragraph of *Lumen gentium* in which the Council explicitly takes up the perspective of poverty in the Church (*LG* 8,3). That paragraph affirms the intrinsic relationship which exists between the Church and poverty and that this is rooted in Christology itself: 'But just as Christ realized the work of redemption in poverty and persecution, so also the Church is called to follow the same route to communicate to men and women the fruits of salvation. Christ Jesus, "was in the form of God ... emptied himself, taking the form of a slave" (Phil. 2.6–7), and for our sake, "being rich, became poor" (2 Cor. 8.9); in the same way also the Church, although it needs human means to pursue its mission, was not constituted to attain earthly glory, but to divulge humility and abnegation to humanity, by means of its example. Christ was sent by the Father "to preach good news to the poor ... to heal those who are of contrite heart" (Luke 4.18), "to seek and save that which is lost" (Luke 19.10).'

A perspective which approximates to that of the Church of the Poor can also be found in the chapter dedicated to economic and social life of *Gaudium et spes* (63–72). The Council was, nevertheless, still a European council.

The impact of the positions taken with regard to the Church of the Poor on Paul VI was nonetheless noteworthy. In a speech made to the Conferences of Saint Vincent of Paul on 9 November 1964 he affirmed that 'you know that today the Church of the Poor is often spoken about ... Certainly that relates to us the evangelical origins of the Church itself, even to the purpose of God in the salvation of the world, the unforgetable and indisputable example of

Christ, who was himself poor and the herald to the poor of his Good News ...'

In the course of the Third Session of the Council (1964) two motions were made to the Conciliar Fathers by the Church of the Poor Group: one concerned evangelical poverty and the other the evangelization of the poor and the world of work. Responding to the first motion, a strong and significant gesture was made by Paul VI: the Pontiff's secretary announced that the Pope would donate his Tiara in order to support the poor. In the celebration of the Eucharist on 13 November 1964 the Pope placed the Tiara on the Altar of Saint Peter. The Tiara was bought by North American Catholics through the agency of Cardinal Spellman of New York, and the money raised was given to the poor in Africa. At the end of the Council there was another gesture: the Pope gave a simple ring to the participating bishops in the Council.

The final action, almost at the end of the Council, on 16 November 1965, was when around 40 bishops of the Church of the Poor movement celebrated the Eucharist in the Catacombs of Saint Domitila and signed a document which came to be known as the Pact of the Catacombs. This was later to be signed by a further 500 bishops.[14] The document detailed in 13 points a commitment on the part of the signatories to a Church of the Poor, including the renunciation of titles which express greatness or power (proposing that the bishops should be called Father), luxurious vestments, luxury cars and houses, and to dedicating time 'to apostolic and pastoral service for individuals and groups of workers and those who are economically weak and underdeveloped'.[15]

Pope Paul VI was not satisfied with the fact that the question of the poor and the Church had not been well developed in the Council. This is seen in a statement to D. Joao Mota, Archbishop of Vitória in Brazil and an active member of the Church of the Poor Group.[16] Before the end of the Council Paul VI requested Lercaro to provide him with an outline response to the question of poverty, with the intention of writing a future encyclical on the subject. Although Lercaro handed over the outline on 19 November 1964, the encyclical was never written.[17] Instead, Paul VI wrote the encyclical *Populorum progressio*, in which he addressed the themes of development and of poverty in the world. In the encyclical, Paul reaffirmed the centrality of the poor in the Mission of Jesus and, moreover, the necessity of the Church developing on the basis of such a central understanding: 'True to the teaching and example of her divine Founder, who cited the preaching of the Gospel to the poor as a sign of

His mission, the Church has never failed to foster the human progress of the nations to which she brings faith in Christ' (*PP* 12). The terms 'poor', 'poor country' and 'poverty' appear 25 times in the encyclical.

III   The Church of the Poor and Latin America

The question of the Church of the Poor was to encounter fertile ground in the post-conciliar environment in Latin America. From the mid-1960s onwards, there arose a variety of religious communities, marking the start of the experience of base ecclesial communities. These are small communities in working-class settings where the people organize themselves ecclesially, read the Bible in community, pray, form links and immerse themselves in the struggle for social transformation, in union with their priests and bishops. These communities mark the beginning of a process which has been called a genuine ecclesiogenesis, the forming of a Church of the Poor deep in the heart of Catholic life and doctrine.[18]

The Second General Conference of the Latin American Bishops took place in Medellín in 1968. Its objective was to apply the Council to the Latin American Church. What happened in Medellín was a full reception not only of the Council, but also of the Poor Church and the Church of the Poor, taking its trajectory from the Pact of the Catacombs and the theological perspective of Lercaro. Document 14 from Medellín specifically welcomes in its entirety the text of the Pact, and the question of the poor does not simply appear as a theme, but as the structuring principle of Christian life and of the Church. This is the context in which liberation theology developed, with Medellín at its roots, not as a theology about a theme (a theology of the poor), but as an all-encompassing systematic theology, which has as its starting point the question of what it means to be a Christian in a continent of the poor, the exploited and the oppressed. It is a theology that sets out to accompany the pastoral practice of a Church which chooses to become poor, to place itself on the side of the poor and commits itself to the process of liberation from every form of oppression and marginalization. Already in Medellín the necessary solidarity with the poor was affirmed.

The literal expression 'Option for the Poor' arose at the beginning of the 1970s and became the fundamental identifying mark of the Latin American Church, so that the Church 'gives a clear preference to the sectors in society which are for whatever reason the poorest, most needy and segregated'.[19]

The Option for the Poor in the Latin American Church has two central meanings: material solidarity with the poor, leading to a change in social position, taking on the perspective of the poor, their interests, pains and anxieties, and implying the commitment with the Church itself to 'material poverty' and the denunciation of institutional structures which produce poverty and oppression (*M* 14,5).

From the 1970s onwards, resistance and opposition to the Church of the Poor and to liberation theology would also grow, being expressed by conservative Catholic sections of society linked to the dominant classes in Latin America. In the case of Brazil, these minorities controlled the discourse and counted on Rome, and decisively from the media, for their support in the context of military dictatorship which dominated the country. In the midst of growing tensions, the hegemonic position of the Brazilian episcopate was to remain strong in its support for base communities, pastoral associations and liberation theology.

The Third General Conference of the Latin American Bishops took place in 1979 in Puebla, now under the papacy of John Paul II. The preparations for Puebla were characterized by intense debate, and the inaugural speech of the new Pontiff was very hesitant in respect of the Church of the Poor. Nevertheless, Puebla reaffirmed the Option for the Poor, adding, however, the word 'Preferential' and stating that it was neither exclusive nor excluding. Such an affirmation was able to reduce the Option merely to the status of a special attention to the poor, making them become once again an object and withdrawing from the Option the character of a structuring principle of the whole Church.

IV   The Option for the Poor from John Paul II to Aparecida

It would fall to John Paul II to adopt the concept of the Option for the Poor in the Social Doctrine of the Church, both in the encyclical *Sollicitudo rei socialis* (42) and in *Centesimus annus* (11,57). The Option for the Poor thus gained a place in the pontifical magisterium, even if this was in a qualified sense. If, on the one hand, the Pontiff, in recognizing that 'the love of the Church for the poor ... is decisive and belongs to its consistent tradition', made a great advance at that time, faced with the conservative positions which deny any privilege for the poor, on the other hand, in

34

his broadening of the concept of 'poor' to include cultural and religious poverty, he detracted from the character of the Option itself (*CA* 57).

The Fourth General Conference of the Latin American Episcopate took place in 1992 in San Domingos. The conservative advance had gained strength, and the preparations for the conference took place in an atmosphere of high tension. Nonetheless the Option for the Poor was clearly reaffirmed in at least seven paragraphs (50, 178–80, 275, 296, 302). The Church of the Poor was weakened, given that the proposed pastoral agenda diluted the Option and its character as a structuring principle.

The Fifth General Conference of the Latin American Bishops took place in Aparecida in 2007, now in the papacy of Benedict XVI. In his opening speech Benedict XVI referred to the Option in the following terms. '[The] Preferential Option for the Poor is implicit in Christological faith in as much as God became poor for our sake, in order to enrich us by means of his poverty.' The Option for the Poor was restated at Aparecida (128, 397, 398, 399). The poor appear in at least 86 paragraphs. It can be asserted that the Church of the Poor had been partially reclaimed, in the sense of a structural vision of reality, along with the denunciation of mechanisms of oppression and exclusion and the recognition of different forms of poverty on the continent.

Shortly afterwards, following the election of Pope Francis, the question of the Church of the Poor has taken centre stage in the Supreme Magisterium of the Church. Francis reaffirms the Option for the Poor and the theme of the Church of the Poor and for the 'poor' in its original sense, as found in Lercaro, the Pact of the Catacombs, Medellín and in subsequent Latin American praxis. It is a structuring Option for the Church which, as the Sacrament of the Poor Christ, Messiah, eschatological Judge, is the Church of all, sent for the salvation of the world. It cannot be anything else other than the Church of the Poor.

Notes

1. Cf. L. J. Suenens, *Aux origins du Concile Vatican II*, NRT 107/1 (1985), pp. 3–21, p. 17.
2. See the article published by Alfred Sauvy in the French journal *L'observateur* on 14 August 1952.
3. See R. Gil Benumeya, 'Tradición y actualidad em la evolución internacional del socialismo árabe', *Revista de Política Internacional,* 89 (1967), pp. 37–54; also E. Almeida, 'O Pan-Africanismo e a formação da OUA', *Revista Geo-paisage,* 6/12 (2007), www.feth.ggf.br/África.htm. For Latin America, E. Faletto, 'Los años 60 y el tema de la dependência', *Estudos avançados,* 12.33 (1998), São Paulo.

4. Cf. A. Ricardi, 'Chiesa e povertã in etã contemporanea', in Annibale di Francia, *La Chiesa e la povertã*, Rome, 1992, pp. 151–70.
5. See the 1974 work of W. Buhlmann, *O Terceiro Mundo e a Terceira Igreja*, São Paulo, 1976.
6. The text was subsequently published as P. Gauthier, *Les pauvres, Jésus et l'Église*, Paris, 1963.
7. Veja-se C. Lorefice, *Dossetti e Lercaro: La Chiesa povera e dei poveri nella prospecttiva del Concilio Vaticano II*, Milano, 2011, pp. 136–7.
8. The texts are published in G. Lercaro, *Per la Forza dello Spirito: Discursi Conciliari*, Bologna, 2014.
9. Lercaro, *Per la Forza*, p. 129.
10. Lercaro, *Per la Forza*, p.147.
11. Lercaro, *Per la Forza*, p. 146.
12. Lercaro, *Per la Forza*, p. 149.
13. Lorefice, *Dossetti e Lercaro*, p. 260.
14. Some refer to this as Schema 14, 'The schema concerning the poor', to be added to the other schemas of the Council and bringing it to its completion. Cf. B. Klopenpurg, *Concílio Vaticano II: Vol V, Quarta Sessão*, Petrópolis, 1966, pp. 526–8.
15. The document can be found in *Concilium* 124, 1977/4.
16. Cf. P. Gauthier, *El Evangelio de la Justicia y los Pobres*, Salamanca, 1969, p. 200.
17. Lercaro, *Per la Forza*, pp. 151–63.
18. D. Barbé and E. Retumba, *Retrato de uma Comunidade de Base*, Petrópolis, 1970.
19. J. Lois, *Teologia de la Liberacion: Opcion por los Pobres*, Madrid, 1988, p. 336.

The Way Ahead

CARLOS MESTERS AND FRANCISCO OROFINO

This article seeks to outline the new paradigms for the popular reading of the Bible in Latin America, starting from an analysis of what has been done in the last 50 years. It highlights the various challenges presented by the situation in Latin America and the way these influence this approach to the Bible.

In an attempt to cheer up the exiles, the prophet Jeremiah gave some advice to those who were undergoing the harsh experience of exile: 'Set up road markers for yourself, make yourself signposts; consider well the highway, the road by which you went' (Jer. 31.21). The present article tries to do precisely that. We were asked to 'indicate the new paradigms Latin American interpretation of the Bible has to face'. Our intention is to take a quick look at the path we have been travelling since the 1970s until today in the hope that as we look backwards, over the journey already completed, we may be able to see the way ahead.

It is the people's faith that welcomes the Bible as what it really is, the Word of God for us. Obviously this Word of God becomes part of our recent history, of the various moments in which, here in Brazil, we have lived, worked, built, loved, suffered, shared and been a community. There were many moments. Some were very intense, such as the transition from the military dictatorship to the new Constitution (1995–8). Others were moments of deep frustration, when the elected governments embarked on neoliberal policies and disrupted the popular movement. Gradually we came to see that this process of contextualized insertion of the Word is not static, but profoundly dynamic. This demands a constant revision of our way of working with the Word. But what we really discovered in this whole process is that it is only possible to work with the Word of God if you let the Word of God work on you. As

37

a result we have to record that we have also changed a lot! Thank God!

This article, inevitably, reflects our journey within CEBI (The Centre for Biblical Studies). CEBI was created and exists to be at the service of the popular reading of the Bible. In the 1970s, in conversations with groups of pastoral workers that led to the creation of CEBI, some people said, 'The Bible is the petrol hidden in the popular movement!' CEBI was born to explain, develop, energize and systematize this reading of the Bible that the people were already doing in small groups of poor people. Some of these groups met in rural areas, others in the outskirts of the cities, which began to swell as a result of the process of galloping urbanization in the period of the military dictatorship's 'economic miracle' (1964–85).

When we talk about 'popular reading', we mean the liberating interpretation practised in the Church base communities (CEBs). This service to popular reading is the determining factor in the different methods that were adopted by CEBI in the course of time. These methods are the product of the constant interaction between popular reading and the evolution of the popular movement and popular education in recent years.

I   Some remarks about the popular movement

It is clear that in these years of our biblical journey many things have changed in the social movements and the popular organizations. In its own way, the population gradually found new ways of organizing and expressing its quests, dreams and desires. In the 1970s, the main emphasis was on the protests and demonstrations against the military dictatorship and high prices. Today, in the fight against the rule of neoliberalism there is a tendency to work through solidarity networks and social networks on the internet. Today we find a whole range of proposals that can be local (refuse collectors' cooperatives), regional (the movement in defence of the semi-arid regions), national (the law on political corruption) and international (ecological NGOs). In linking these various movements the new means of communication and information via the internet play an important role. This communications activity produces and develops new techniques and new skills in the popular movement. Its aim is the 'empowerment' of people and groups. This means that its main goal is to strengthen the effective participation of people in civil society to break the hold of the neoliberal financial system. Dominating the main communications media

(TV, newspapers and weekly magazines), neoliberalism is able to impose its trinity: individualism, consumerism and privatization of goods and services. The successive World Social Forums have given visibility to this vast number of small localized projects and struggles, showing that the motivation and mobilization of people depends largely on affinity and a localized vision of problems.

This explains why, in contrast to the 1970s and 1980s, there now exist new forms of action and association within the popular movement. There is not such a quest for a large association bringing together large numbers of people such as there was in the Brazilian campaign for direct elections to Congress after the dictatorship. What we have today is one-off, local mobilization, based on a very specific local problem, which mobilizes both those directly affected and various groups of sympathizers. Generally, mobilization is a response to an appeal made by a national or international NGO calling people in what is called 'citizen participation'.

All this calls for a revision of our biblical work. When CEBI began, at the end of the 1970s, there were a large number of popular social movements linked in opposition to the military regime. Our biblical interpretation mainly reached the grass-roots movements present in the Christian churches and inspired by liberation theology. With the fall of the military regime and the subsequent organization of Brazilian democracy through the 1988 Constitution, this situation obviously changed a lot. The mass demonstrations calling for political participation and democratic freedoms disappeared. After all, we are now in a democratic, representative system; there is no more need for political groups to take refuge in churches. The Workers' Party (PT), organized out of the churches' social movements, trade unions and intellectuals, was the political channel for popular demands. The movements saw many of their demands find their way into the text of the new Constitution, though much remained merely on paper.

Nevertheless demobilization had begun. And it has continued to this day, even though demonstrators have come on to the streets from time to time, as in the calls for the impeachment of President Collor or the battle against the neoliberal privatizations (1994–2000), or the demonstrations of June–July 2013 against the rise in urban transport fares and protests against the big construction projects associated with the 2014 World Cup and the 2016 Olympics. On top of this, there was the huge political frustration produced by the PT's years in government from 2003, when their neoliberal policies reinforced the process of wealth concentration.

If we want to find the new paradigms for a popular reading of the Bible in Latin America, we have to focus on some issues that are mobilizing people today and putting new life into social and popular movements:

(a) **Land** is the issue that is most visible nationally. Of the roughly 20 rural social movements in Brazil, the Landless Movement (MST) is best known because it has the best communications strategy. But we cannot forget the struggles of the indigenous and the Afro-Brazilian *quilombola* groups for the confirmation of the legal protection of their reserves.

(b) **The Ethics in Politics Movement and the Faith and Politics groups**. This broad alliance has had great victories, such as the overthrow of Collor, the popular referendums against the privatization of the Vale do Rio Doce mining company and the foreign debt and the laws on political corruption. But it also suffered defeats, as in the referendum on gun control.

(c) **The growth of the indigenous movements** was stimulated by the celebrations of the 500th anniversary of the arrival of the whites (1992–2000). This movement won its greatest victory with the demarcation of Raposa-Serra do Sol reserve in Roraima and the recuperation of the lands of the Pataxó people in the south of Bahia. Here in Brazil it is the indigenous who put up the greatest resistance to the development policies sponsored by the PT. It is disappointing to see how little attention a popular government gives to the indigenous question.

(d) **The battle of Afro-Brazilians** to become more visible in Brazilian society, particularly in education with their victory in securing university quotas and in the battle for the *quilombola* lands, the territories established by escaped slaves.

(e) **The big demonstrations of homosexual people and their supporters**, which brought thousands of people on to the Gay Pride marches and led to victory in the recognition of unions between people of the same sex.

(f) **The various ecological crusades**. Since the 1992 UN environment conference in Rio de Janeiro, a popular struggle has become established over ecological issues. Resistance to mega-projects, to big dams and to agro-business are mobilizing and uniting many resistance groups, as was demonstrated at Rio+20 in June 2012.

(g) **New scientific discoveries** that modify people's outlook and attitudes: information technology, biotechnology, quantum physics, nanotechnology, etc.

(h) **The face of the poor as presented in the Aparecida document**. In the face of the challenges of neoliberal globalization, the Aparecida document (paras 64–5) invited us to develop a 'different sort of globalization', marked by solidarity, justice and respect for human rights. The document, following the tradition of the previous General Conferences of Latin American bishops, then invites us to 'contemplate the faces of those who suffer' and gives a long list of men and women who suffer as a result of neoliberal policies, a 'globalization without solidarity that has a negative impact on the poorest sectors'. Among this long list of people affected, it is worthwhile to single out a few:

- The first face mentioned is that of the *indigenous communities*, those who suffer most from the advance of agribusiness, dams and large infrastructure projects.
- Then come *women*, excluded by their sex, race or socio-economic situation.
- Next are *young people*, who are given a low-quality education that excludes them from a labour market that increasingly requires academic or professional qualifications.
- *Elderly people*, who, apart from feeling excluded by the productive system, feel abandoned by their families and have few resources for the medication and medical support they need.
- Those who are trying to survive in the *informal economy*: the poor, the unemployed, migrants, the displaced, landless agricultural workers.
- *Victims of human trafficking*: child prostitution, sexual slaves of both sexes, victims of organ trafficking, workers enslaved through debt.
- The *huge prison population*, victims of police without proper training and selective repression that mainly targets poor black young people.

The Aparecida document ends this exposition by stressing that 'this is not simply a phenomenon of exploitation or oppression, but something new. The excluded are not only "exploited", but "superfluous" and "throw-away" people. This is the starting point for coming to terms with the period in which we are living. Contemplating the faces of the "throw-away people", the victims of an inhuman economic system, we can understand Pope Francis' cry in *Evangelii gaudium*: "This economy kills!... This is exclusion" (*EG* 53).

But despite all the technological, political, social and economic advances, which place Brazil among the eight most powerful economies in the world, we are still a tremendously unequal country. Many groups are still dealing with the struggles of the 1970s and 1980s, work, health care, transport, education, housing and food. These are the new challenges that lead us to ask what is the role of the new historical actors, that collection summed up in the word 'people', which defines the popular movement. The question we are left with is: what sort of biblical reading can we offer that will cope with these new challenges? Biblical interpretation is being influenced by the very same challenges as the popular movement. It is a reciprocal influence and a reciprocal enrichment.

II New challenges from the popular reading

The popular reading of the Bible brings some very important challenges that need to be considered. Here is a list of five:

1. Feminist or gendered reading

This reading questions and relativizes the centuries-old macho reading that has enabled the churches to maintain the patriarchal system. Gendered reading cannot be dismissed as a passing fad or one of the many exegetical curiosities that are really not very important. It is one of the most important features emerging within the popular reading of the Bible, and its range is much greater than might appear at first sight. In Brazil, it has acquired greater importance because of the overwhelming number of women who take an active part in Bible groups and in many places are the mainstay of the people's struggle. In CEBI, a large number of women trainers have qualified in the last few years, and they are taking forward gendered reading, not as a new area, but as a feature that should mark all the popular reading we engage in.

2. How to deal with the fact of fundamentalism?

In the Bible study meetings run by CEBI, which are open to people from the various sectors of the life of the churches, the following phenomenon is becoming increasingly common. The study and interpretation of the Bible are done in a clearly liberationist perspective. But in the liturgies, the group conversations and the question sessions a different interpretative attitude comes up in which fundamentalism is mixed with liberation theology. This is especially common among young people. How are we to explain this? Where does it come from? Is it from contact with the conservative view, the charismatic view, with the Pentecostals? Or does it perhaps also come from inadequacies in the liberationist attitude to the Bible? Or does it come from something even deeper that is changing in humanity's subconscious? After all, the fact of fundamentalism exists not only in the Christian churches, but also in other religions, Jewish, Moslem, Buddhist. There are even forms of secular fundamentalism. Fundamentalism is a threat. It separates the text from the rest of the people's life and history and turns it into an absolute as the only manifestation of the Word of God. It implies that life, the people's history, the community, have nothing more to say about God and God's will. Fundamentalism cancels out the action of the Word of God in life. It is the total absence of critical consciousness. It distorts the meaning of the Bible and encourages moralism, individualism, political conservatism and spiritualism in interpretation. It is an alienated vision that suits the people's oppressors and prevents the oppressed from becoming aware of the iniquity of the system set up and maintained by those in power. In the Catholic Church, for the first time, the 1993 Vatican document *The Interpretation of the Bible in the Church* strongly criticized fundamentalism as something harmful that doesn't sufficiently respect the meaning of the Bible.

3. The search for spirituality and our method of interpretation

All over the place you hear and feel the desire for greater depth, for a sense of mysticism, for spirituality. The Bible can certainly be a response to this desire. The Word of God has two fundamental dimensions. On the one hand, it brings light. In this sense, it can contribute to clarify ideas, expose false ideologies and impart a more critical outlook. On the other hand, it brings strength. From this point of view it can encourage people, instil courage and bring happiness, since it is the creative force that produces new possibilities, gives birth to the people, creates facts, generates love. Unfortunately, in pastoral practice these two aspects of the Word are often separated: on one side we have the charismatic movements, on the other the liberation movements. The charismatics are big on prayer, but very often they lack critical vision and tend towards a fundamentalist, moralizing and individualistic view of the Bible. As a result, their prayer often lacks a real grounding in the text and in real life. Liberation movements, for their part, are big on critical consciousness but sometimes lack perseverance and faith when they have to face human situations and relationships between people that, in an objective analysis, contribute nothing to the transformation of society. Sometimes they have some difficulty in seeing the point of long hours spent in prayer with no immediate result.

4. The culture of the first peoples

We need to break the hold of Bible reading as an instrument of colonization. In the myth of Tucumã, which gives the Indians of the Amazon region their explanation of the origin of evil in the world, responsibility for the origin of evils is not woman, but man. In a Bible study meeting someone asked, 'Why don't we use our myths instead of the myths of the Hebrew people?' There was no reply. The same question was raised at a Bible course in Bolivia. The participants, almost all Aymaras, asked: 'Why just use the Bible? Our stories are more beautiful, less macho and better known!' The religious of Asia, more ancient than ours, have been raising the same questions for a number of years. What is the value of our history and our culture? Could they not act as our Old Testament, where we could find hidden the promises God made to our ancestors, and where we could find our law to act as 'our tutor until Christ came' (Gal. 3.14)? The gospel did not come to replace the Old Testament, but to complete it and make clear all its meaning (Matt. 5.17). The Old Testament of the people of Israel is the 'canon' or inspired standard that helps us to understand and discover this deeper dimension of our culture and history, of our Old Testament. In this respect, the various attempts at an indigenous, black and gendered reading of the Bible are very important.

Many people ask, 'But what do we do about the Bible's outdated view of the universe?' Here it's worthwhile having another look at a remark by Clement of Alexandria, a wise African from the fourth century CE who lived in the city of Alexandria in the north of Egypt. He said: 'God saved the Jews in a Jewish way, the Greeks in a Greek way and the barbarians in a barbarian way.' We could carry on: 'and the Brazilians in a Brazilian way, the Argentines in an Argentine way, the Latinos in a Latino way and so on'. The Jews, the Greeks and the barbarians, each in their own time and their own culture, through their stubborn faith and in the middle of the many crises of their history, were able to discover the signs of God's loving presence in their lives. In the same way we too are being challenged to do what they did in their time, that is, discover the same presence of God in our culture, express it in the forms of our understanding of the universe, to create new forms of celebration that correspond to the deepest desires of our hearts. We are challenged to radiate this faith to others as amazing Good News for human life, to do what Jesus did in his time, to pass on God's Good News.

5. *The need for deeper study of the Bible in Latin America*

The communities' journey moves on and goes to new depths. Gradually, from the heart of this popular practice, a new interpretative attitude is arising that is not new, but very old. It has a need to be legitimated both by the tradition of the churches and by exegetical research. The reading that is done from the situation of the poor and from the perspective of the cause of the poor has its own demands. As it moves forward, the desire for a deeper understanding of biblical studies grows. There are many popular educators who would like to have some knowledge of the biblical languages, they would like to have a better understanding of the economic, political, social and ideological context in which the Bible emerged, they would like to take into the Bible the questions that trouble the people as they try to live out their faith. There is a shortage of academic tutors able to respond to the increasing demand for biblical training from the popular tutors and to meet the new problem being created by the immense rise of fundamentalism.

III   Conclusion: learning from the Book of Revelation

The Book of Revelation is a wide-ranging analysis of the situation faced by the small Christian communities at the end of the first century of our era. With great objectivity and creativity, the book focuses on the two great threats to the lives of these communities (Rev. 13.1–18). The great adversary of God's project, the dragon, calls up two beasts to destroy the community of the saints. The first beast comes up out of the sea. It is a violent killer. This first beast is easily identifiable: it is the Roman empire, which now has power over everything and everyone. In the 1970s and 1980s, here in Latin America, we faced the same beast and knew its name, the national security state. Many throughout Latin America fell in this conflict and we have many martyrs who were 'taken captive and killed by the sword' (Rev. 13.10). Our methods of Bible reading were forged in the fight against this first beast.

But things changed, and a second beast came. This second beast appears on the land, from within groups and communities. It looks like a lamb, but when it speaks it is the dragon itself. It performs great miracles that leave everyone amazed and bewitched. It seduces humanity with images and prodigies and owns a brand that allows all, great and small, slaves and free, rich and poor, to buy, sell and consume (Rev. 13.16). For the communities of the first century, this beast was the spirit of the Roman Empire, circulating as coins, money. For us here in Latin America, this second beast is neoliberalism, with its individualistic ideology that breaks down the unity of communities; with its consumer offers it has everyone falling, amazed and bewitched, on electronic devices and apps. But its main weapon is its ideology of the ultimate goal: prosperity, victory and miracles, cures and getting rich.

Our reading of the Bible came up with methods to deal with the first beast. Have we worked out how to deal with the second?

Translated by Francis McDonagh

The Dignity the Poor Demand after Liberation in South Africa

GERALD O. WEST

This article addresses the place of dignity in South Africa 20 years after political liberation through a close examination of the Abahlali baseMjondolo movement, a homeless peoples' movement. The author explores 'the socio-economic and theological dimensions of dignity, as well as the role of the socially engaged biblical scholar in offering critical resources to recover the prophetic trajectory of dignity's revolt in the Bible'. He concludes that what 'connected the Jesus community was not an ethnic ethic, but a socio-economic ethic' and offers this insight as a critical component for the struggle of the poor in South Africa.

I Introduction

In the recent South African film *Son of Man*, a re-telling of the gospel story of Jesus set in post-liberation South Africa, Jesus addresses the crowd in a shack settlement. Standing on top of a VIP (Ventilated Improved Pit latrine) toilet, Jesus delivers this film's version of Matthew's Sermon on the Mount (or part of it) (0:47.35).[1] While armed soldiers loiter in the background and a military helicopter hovers overhead, Jesus says (in isiXhosa): 'My people, we have deliberately chosen to operate openly. Let us work together, because through collective dialogue we can penetrate the deafest of ears.' As the crowd roars its approval, he continues, saying, 'It feels like we are defeated. We need to act like a movement to ensure that each of us is treated with dignity.'

While there is much in this film that worries me,[2] the moment when Jesus reminds the people of their dignity rings true both to our context and the Gospels. Jesus, both in this film and in portions of the Gospel

47

accounts, recognizes that dignity resides both in the individual and in their collaborative action in the public realm. In this article, I explore how 'dignity' has emerged as a central concept in the post-liberation struggles of the poor in South Africa. The socio-economic and theological dimensions of dignity are analysed, as well as the role of the socially engaged biblical scholar in offering critical resources to recover a prophetic trajectory of dignity's revolt in the Bible.

II   The Bible's prophetic trajectory

Within biblical scholarship across a range of contextual sites there have been regular attempts to analyse the contending voices within biblical texts. Norman Gottwald's work on early 'Israel' was among the pioneering work in this area, and although the focus of this work had a strong historical and sociological emphasis,[3] in his later work he did use this socio-historical analysis to discern contending voices in the literary productions themselves.[4] Robert Coote's work on Amos was perhaps the most sustained project of this kind, including socio-historical, literary and even theological analysis.[5] Both Gottwald's and Coote's work was taken up by South African biblical scholar Itumeleng Mosala,[6] and his contribution produced a seismic shift in South African and North American Black Theology, inaugurating what Tinyiko Maluleke refers to as a second wave of South African Black Theology,[7] in which the Bible is no longer a mono-vocal resource on the side of the liberation struggle.

Finding echoes in the film *Son of Man*, what Richard Horsley reconstructs, for example, as the ideology of the Jesus community found in Mark and the traditions ascribed to Q within Matthew and Luke, is in continuity with Walter Brueggemann's 'prophetic trajectory', 'a movement of protest which is situated among the disinherited and which articulates its theological vision in terms of a God who decisively intrudes, even against seemingly impenetrable institutions and orderings' and stands over against what Brueggemann refers to as the 'consolidatory trajectory', 'a movement of consolidation which is situated among the established and secure and which articulates its theological vision in terms of a God who faithfully abides and sustains on behalf of the present ordering'.[8]

As Horsley argues, the communities of the Jesus movement thought of themselves as 'a new social order',[9] but a social order that both breaks with consolidatory formations and stands in continuity with prophetic forces. Indeed, Horsley's particular contribution lies in his recognition and analysis of the contending nature of this 'renewal' project. In a world full of various tensions, the 'fundamental conflict in Jewish Palestine was ... between the ruling groups, on the one hand, and the bulk of the people, on the other'.[10] What connected the Jesus community was not an ethnic ethic, but a socio-economic ethic.

A distinctive contribution of Horsley's analysis is his argument that the primary ethic of the Jesus movement and their renewal project was an internal ethic. The 'sermon' material in Luke 12.22–31/Matthew 6.25–33 is a good example of this, calling for an internal ethic of the renewal of reciprocity. This is not primarily an external ethic, directed to those outside the community, but first and foremost an internal 'local' socio-economic ethic, focused on building a community of solidarity and resistance.[11]

It is the primacy and priority of an internal community ethic that the *Son of Man* film emphasizes. What the *Son of Man* film makes overt is the implicit place of dignity in this ethic. In the next section of this article, I analyse the central place that dignity has come to hold in post-liberation social movements.

III   Abahlali baseMjondolo

The place of dignity in our contemporary struggle, nearly 20 years after political liberation, is clearly expressed in the Abahlali baseMjondolo movement. On 19 March 2005, a group of black shack dwellers barricaded a major road in Durban, KwaZulu-Natal, South Africa. Like so many other 'service delivery protests',[12] a sign of our times, this action was a protest against the failure of the state to deliver housing for the Kennedy Road shack dwellers. As bulldozers moved in to level 'their "Promised Land"'(and the biblical image is theirs),[13] the community acted, barricading Umgeni Road with their bodies and burning tyres. More than 700 shack dwellers participated in this protest action, and despite a vigorous police response, two days later, on 21 March, Human Rights Day (and the anniversary of the 1960 Sharpeville massacre), more than 1,000 demonstrated.

As Nigel Gibson argues, 'Their demands were far from revolutionary; they were the demands of loyal citizens making reasonable requests, borne of their citizenship, for inclusion in the "new South Africa": for housing, safety, health care and political representation.'[14] For Abahlali, says Gibson, 'democracy was not about an election every five years, but about day-to-day life that included reciprocity, caring and the inclusion of those who had been systematically excluded and told they were too stupid to understand'.[15] In the words of S'bu Zikode, an Abahlali organic intellectual, 'Our struggle is for moral questions, as compared to the political questions as such. It is more about justice. Is it good for shack dwellers to live in mud like pigs, as they are living?', he asks by way of illustration. 'Why do I live in a cardboard house if there are people who are able to live in a decent house? So it is a moral question.'[16] It is for this reason that Abahlali has consistently refuted the discourse of 'service delivery'; 'they insist instead that their demands are about "being human"'; indeed, in the words of Zikode, 'the struggle is the human being'.[17] In Gibson's language, which resonates with Horsley's analysis of the early Jesus movement, 'Abahlalism is a culture of sharing that is rooted in the ideas of community and reciprocity found in the long struggle against apartheid.'[18]

It is not surprising, therefore, that notions of 'dignity' have assumed such a central place in the discourse of Abahlali. 'We fought, died and voted for this government,' says Zikode, 'so that we could be free and have decent lives.'[19] One of the major goals of Abahlali, argues Gibson, building on Zikode's analysis, 'is a kind of moral revolution, the creation of a society where the poor will be treated as human being[s] with minds of their own'. As Zikode likes to say, cites Gibson, 'We are poor in life, not in mind.'[20]

Abahlali embodies, both in their community action and their community reflection, James Scott's understanding of resistance to domination. Scott allocates an important role to human dignity. Indeed, Scott admits that he privileges 'the issues of dignity and autonomy, which have typically been seen as secondary to material exploitation'.[21] No matter how severe the domination, and Scott focuses on extreme forms of domination, dignity always demands a response to domination. Like Abahlali, Scott recognizes that the poor are not poor in mind. Central to his analysis is the recognition that subordinate classes 'are less constrained at the level of thought and ideology, since they can in secluded settings speak with comparative safety, and more constrained at the level of political action and struggle, where the daily exercise of power sharply limits the options available to them'.[22] What political liberation has brought to South Africa is the political space for the hidden transcript to enter the public realm. And Abahlali has embraced this space, giving a fulsome account of dignity's revolt to the state's 'systemic neglect'.[23]

IV Dignity's revolt

John Holloway, like Scott and Abahlali, locates dignity at the heart of social movements of the marginalized.[24] Beginning with the self-evident assertion that dignity is 'the refusal to accept humiliation and dehumanization', he interrogates both the 'is' and the 'is not' of dignity. 'Dignity, understood as a category of struggle, is a tension which points beyond itself. The assertion of dignity implies the present negation of dignity. Dignity, then, is the struggle against the denial of dignity, the struggle for the realization of dignity. Dignity is and is not: it is the struggle against its own negation.'[25] 'Dignity is the cry of "here we are!"'[26]

Echoing Zikode, Holloway argues that dignity 'is an assault on the separation of morality and politics and of the private and the public ... The assertion of dignity is neither a moral nor a political claim: it is rather an attack on the separation of politics and morality that allows formally democratic regimes all over the world to co-exist with growing levels of poverty and social marginalization.'[27] Dignity encapsulates, continues Holloway, 'the rejection of the separation of the personal and the political', and the revolt of dignity 'derives its strength from the uniting of dignities'. 'Dignity resonates. As it vibrates, it sets off vibrations in other dignities, an unstructured, possibly discordant resonance.'[28]

Dignity is agentive; dignity is more a verb than a noun. In the words of a joint statement by Abahlali baseMjondolo, the Rural Network and the Unemployed People's Movement, 'Dignity is the road, and it is the destination.'[29]

V People's theology

Organized social movements like Abahlali baseMjondolo represent a call to socially engaged biblical scholars and theologians who stand with the traditions of liberation theology to enter into solidarity with them and to do theology with them. The revised second edition (1986) of the *Kairos* Document prepares the way for us, making a distinction between 'people's theology' and 'prophetic theology'. 'People's theology' is organic to the organized social movements of the poor. 'Prophetic theology' is the more systematic representation of this embodied theology in the public realm.[30] There can be no prophetic theology without there first being a people's theology, according to the *Kairos* Document.

Sadly, however, this priority, with people's theology preceding prophetic theology, has been neglected since our political liberation. But as Abahlali reminds us, the need has not diminished, it simply has a different face.

And the resources remain. The Institute for Contextual Theology (ICT) and the work of Albert Nolan, together with the associated work of the Ujamaa Centre,[31] have been instrumental in both theorizing and facilitating this people's theology/prophetic theology process of doing theology.[32] So there is a guiding methodology for doing theology 'with' social movements within the kind of solidarity envisaged by Abahlali, if we are prepared to heed the call. The 'raw material' is already there; people's theology is already present in the dignity discourse of Abahlali.

If we return to the inaugural protests that gave birth to Abahlali baseMjondolo, people's theology was present. In welcoming the 14 who had been arrested by the police and held for ten days, 'Zikode, together with Nonhlanhla Mzombe and other community activists, organized a welcome home party for the 14, at which Zikode held the crowd rapt with the following affirmation of their actions. "The first Nelson Mandela," he explained, "was Jesus Christ. The second was Nelson Rolihlahla Mandela. The third Nelson Mandela are the poor people of the world".'[33] Reflecting on this people's theology, Nigel Gibson offers a further (though non-theological) articulation, saying: 'The resonance was clear. The poor weren't Christ, but Christ was the first Mandela, the first liberator who articulated a new heaven and a new earth. Mandela is Christ reborn, grounding liberation firmly on South African soil, his long imprisonment during apartheid a metaphor for the nation, just as his release is identified with the birth of a new South Africa. Yet, the failure of the historical Mandela to liberate South Africa demanded the birth of a new Mandela: the poor themselves ... Subtly criticizing Mandela's historical leadership, the poor were taking matters into their own hands, seeing themselves as the force and reason for their own liberation; they had become their own Mandelas.'[34]

Those of us who are theologians could take this further, for surely S'bu Zikode is saying that Mandela comes/stands in the trajectory of the prophets and Jesus Christ. He is, in some respects, like Christ. But the real Mandela, the second Mandela, has not been fully faithful to this prophetic trajectory,[35] and so another has arisen in the prophetic trajectory of Jesus, the people themselves. Put differently, from the perspective of a biblical scholar, the people (in Abahlali's particular sense of the term) were always at the core of God's project of liberation, with their own organic intellectuals, like Jesus, who gave prophetic expression to the people's theology of each particular era. God's project was always about the people, with the people as the key agents of the project, with God.

VI Dignity after Mandela

While we cannot dispute Mandela's personal legacy, Abahlali demands that this legacy must take structural form. The socio-economic weave of the fabric of our society, they claim, must be constituted by dignity. Sampie Terreblanche reminds us that South Africa has inherited 'a history of inequality'. South Africa's economic system has moved, Terreblanche argues, 'over the past 30 years from one of colonial and racial capitalism to a neo-liberal, first-world, capitalist enclave that is disengaging itself from a large part of the black labour force'. This transformation, he continues, though it has 'coincided with the introduction of a system of representative democracy which is effectively controlled by a black, predominantly African, elite,' still exhibits 'an ominous systemic character'. The common denominator between the old and the new systems, he argues, 'is that part of society was/is systemically and undeservedly enriched, while the majority of the population were/are systemically and undeservedly impoverished – in the old system through systemic exploitation and in the new system through systemic neglect'.[36]

Abahlali locates the centre of this systemic neglect in the refusal to recognize the dignity of the poor and marginalized. And it is the argument of this article that socially engaged biblical scholars cannot participate in this systemic neglect by confining ourselves to the academy. We must, as the liberation tradition demands, do our biblical studies and theology with the organized poor. Among the resources we can offer are the tools to recognize the dignity of marginal voices in our biblical and theological traditions. To recognize that our biblical and theological traditions are themselves internally contested is a significant conceptual contribution in itself.[37] Part of our contribution is to offer (critical) access to these contending voices.

Notes

1. Mark Dornford-May, *Son of Man* (2005).
2. Gerald O. West, 'The Son of Man in South Africa?', in *Son of Man: An African Jesus Film*, eds Richard Walsh, Jeffrey L. Staley and Adele Reinhartz, Sheffield, 2013.

3. Norman K. Gottwald, *The Tribes of Yahweh: A Sociology of the Religion of Liberated Israel, 1250-1050 B.C.*, Maryknoll, NY, 1979.
4. Norman K. Gottwald, *The Hebrew Bible: A Socio-Literary Introduction*, Philadelphia, 1985.
5. Robert B. Coote, *Amos among the Prophets: Composition and Theology*, Philadelphia, 1981.
6. Itumeleng J. Mosala, *Biblical Hermeneutics and Black Theology in South Africa*, Grand Rapids, 1989.
7. Tinyiko S. Maluleke, 'Black Theology as Public Discourse', in *Constructing a Language of Religion in Public Life: Multi-Event 1999 Academic Workshop Papers*, ed. James R. Cochrane, Cape Town, 1998, pp. 60–2.
8. Walter Brueggemann, 'Trajectories in Old Testament Literature and the Sociology of Ancient Israel', in *The Bible and Liberation: Political and Social Hermeneutics*, ed. Norman K. Gottwald and Richard A Horsley, Maryknoll, NY, 1993, p. 202.
9. Richard A. Horsley, *Sociology and the Jesus Movement*, second edn, New York, 1994, p. 122.
10. Horsley, *Sociology and the Jesus Movement*, p. 85.
11. Horsley, *Sociology and the Jesus Movement*, pp. 124–5. See also Sharon D. Welch, *Communities of Resistance and Solidarity: A Feminist Theology of Liberation*, New York, 1985.
12. For a detailed analysis of so-called 'service delivery protests', see the incisive work of Gillian Hart, *Rethinking the South African Crisis: Nationalism, Populism, Hegemony*, Pietermaritzburg, 2013.
13. Gibson uses this phrase, and I have heard it used by a representative of Abahlali, who has worked with the Ujamaa Centre on a common project. Cf. Nigel Gibson, *Fanonian Practices in South Africa: From Steve Biko to Abahlali BaseMjondolo*, New York, 2011, p. 146.
14. Gibson, *Fanonian Practices in South Africa*, p. 148.
15. Gibson, *Fanonian Practices in South Africa*, pp. 156–7.
16. Cited in Gibson, *Fanonian Practices in South Africa*, p. 157.
17. Gibson, *Fanonian Practices in South Africa*, p. 157.
18. Cited in Gibson, *Fanonian Practices in South Africa*, p. 158.
19. Cited in Gibson, *Fanonian Practices in South Africa*, p. 158.
20. Gibson, *Fanonian Practices in South Africa*, p. 158.
21. James C. Scott, *Domination and the Arts of Resistance: Hidden Transcripts*, New Haven, 1990, p. xi.
22. Scott, *Domination and the Arts of Resistance*, p. 91.
23. Sampie Terreblanche, *A History of Inequality in South Africa, 1652–2002*, Pietermaritzburg, 2002, p. 423.
24. John Holloway, 'Dignity's Revolt', http://libcom.org/library/dignitys-revolt-john-holloway. I have chosen to cite this article in the form in which it is represented on the Abahlali website, as part of the 'University of Abahlali baseMjondolo'. The article was published as John Holloway, 'Dignity's Revolt', in *Zapatista! Reinventing Revolution in Mexico*, eds John Holloway and Elíona Peláez, London, 1998, pp. 159–98.
25. http://libcom.org/library/dignitys-revolt-john-holloway.
26. http://libcom.org/library/dignitys-revolt-john-holloway.
27. http://libcom.org/library/dignitys-revolt-john-holloway.
28. http://libcom.org/library/dignitys-revolt-john-holloway. Scott uses a similar image; see Scott, *Domination and the Arts of Resistance*, p. 224.

29. 'The Dignity of the Poor is Vandalized in Many Quarters', http://abahlali.org/node/9478; see also http://hir.harvard.edu/archives/3068.

30. The Kairos Theologians, *The Kairos Document: Challenge to the Church: A Theological Comment on the Political Crisis in South Africa*, revised second edn, Braamfontein, 1986, pp. 34–5, note 15; Gary S. D. Leonard (ed.), *The Kairos Documents*, Pietermaritzburg, 2011, p. 63, note 15.

31. Gerald O. West, 'Locating "Contextual Bible Study" within Biblical Liberation Hermeneutics and [Alongside] Intercultural Biblical Hermeneutics', *HTS Teologiese Studies/Theological Studies*, 70.1 (2014).

32. Albert Nolan, 'Kairos Theology', in John W. de Gruchy and Charles Villa-Vicencio (eds), *Doing Theology in Context: South African Perspectives*, Cape Town, 1994, pp. 212–18; Albert Nolan, 'Work, the Bible, Workers, and Theologians: Elements of a Workers' Theology', *Semeia* 73 (1996), pp. 213–20; James R. Cochrane, 'Questioning Contextual Theology', in McGlory T. Speckman and Larry T. Kaufmann (eds), *Towards an Agenda for Contextual Theology: Essays in Honour of Albert Nolan*, Pietermaritzburg, 2001, pp. 67–86.

33. 'The Third Nelson Mandela', http://abahlali.org/node/302.

34. Gibson, *Fanonian Practices in South Africa*, p. 147.

35. I invoke here Walter Brueggemann's sense of 'trajectory'; see Brueggemann, 'Trajectories in Old Testament Literature and the Sociology of Ancient Israel', in Norman K. Gottwald and Richard Horsley (eds), *The Bible and Liberation: Political and Social Hermeneutics*, Maryknoll, NY, 1993, pp. 201–26.

36. Terreblanche, *A History of Inequality in South Africa*, pp. 422–3.

37. See Cheryl B. Anderson, *Ancient Laws and Contemporary Controversies: The Need for Inclusive Biblical Interpretation*, Oxford, 2009.

The Fruits of a Friendship with Those who are Marginalized

ETIENNE GRIEU SJ (SÈVRES JESUITS)

When the churches allow themselves to be touched by those who are 'outsiders', they experience the essence of what it is to be spiritual and human. This opens the way for an involvement in the public sphere which does not think first of defending set positions, but is disturbed out of complacency by those who are usually ignored. The churches speak, act, and make themselves vulnerable, because the message they carry calls them to this work. It is in fact a very vigorous way in which to contribute to the common good.

In a globalized world, daily life tends to always be ruled by the same simplistic values, like efficiency, profitability and competitiveness. The ubiquity of these values, made even more formidable because they claim to be universal, has become problematic, excluding those in our society who are unable to measure up. Who can challenge them? How can they be limited and resisted? What can we lean on? There are four contenders.

The loudest group is that of 'religion' in general. Its authority comes from a transcendent higher power, located by its very definition outside of globalization. However, when this higher power is called upon as a legislator, responsible for reshaping society, it is immediately interpreted as wearing the mask of violence. Religions cannot content themselves with appealing to the transcendent in order to criticize the powers that be, as their message is then immediately discredited. Their first challenge is to take into account the context of the values of democracy in order to succeed in making their voices heard. This requires all authority, whatever that might be, to agree to submit to the debate with its proposals, including

56

those relating to the way in which we organize how we live together. It challenges all those who claim to place themselves outside the scope of contradiction.

Cultural and national entities are a second candidate for withstanding the implacable laws of the uniformity of globalization and its consequences. They speak on behalf of heritage, opening paths of reflection considered relevant for today. However, these cultural entities, protective of their history while being anxious about disappearing, may freeze or harden. To survive, their traditions of language, thought and artistic creativity may simply repeat themselves, or even become aggressive. Fixed in the past or manipulated, they then become unable to speak to the world today.

A third contender has emerged recently: future generations who are fighting to live on Earth. Located outside our conversations, they only have the voice that we imagine them to have. Hence the weakness of that voice.

Paradoxically, no doubt, the fourth contender who can challenge a world with ruthless rules is the one relating to those who are disqualified and kept off the playing field. This includes those who cannot get into the game in order to have effective and profitable conversations, because of disability, poverty, exploitation, and all that does not allow them to develop their potential. Misfortune has befallen them or was transmitted from generation to generation. It has locked them in lives of misery. These men, these women, and these children, live the humiliation of being regarded as 'useless to the world'. Kept out of the positions of power where they can make decisions, without the possibility of expressing themselves, they become invisible.

Faced with a globalization which was built for the powerful, the Christian churches can offer real critical perspective, provided they make a covenant with the poor, learning from them and rediscovering their own treasure working for and alongside them. Avoiding addressing the world in the name of a transcendent superpower, the voice of the Church can have an authority which comes from familiarity with a difficult reality to grasp, a reality located outside the usual frameworks. This reality may, in a sense, be described as 'other-worldly'. This reality, which frightens people, is actually where theology takes a prominent place. This is why, for the churches, making a covenant with 'those who are marginalized' becomes both a way to take part in public debate and a way to make the gospel heard. This requires them to be changed, moved, disturbed and shaken up by the weak and suffering. To demonstrate the path that the churches need to take, we will begin with the description of a recent event and discover therein the lessons that the churches need to learn if they are to listen to the voices of those who are on the outside. Then, in the light of the gospel and of what we discover, we will suggest how the Church can open up.

I The authority of the voice no one listens to

In 2013, 12,000 people from all the dioceses of France gathered in Lourdes around the theme 'Serving the communion'. A quarter of them were living in very precarious circumstances. At the opening of the assembly, called 'Diaconia', which was the culmination of two years of work in the diocesan churches, participants marked by a personal experience of poverty shared the fruits of their journey. Their common voice set the tone of the event, of which the following is a brief excerpt: 'Together, we can change things and make it clear that the Church is not reserved for certain people. Together we will build another road, another experience, so that there is dialogue and attentiveness in our meetings, and when we leave church, we will put into practice what we have spoken about. Diaconia could be the beginning of something new: awakening the Church to another perspective, that is to say, following Christ in his way of being alongside the very poorest. Because Jesus himself walked the same paths as the poor.'

With these few sentences, these people living in great difficulty invited the public to see in their lives a new beginning: the awakening of the Church to a rediscovery of Christ as the one who is bound to the poorest, a key insight without which the Church is threatened with apathy and complacency. What they had to say was received as authoritative. They reminded the Church of her vocation. Judging by the effect on the very large assembly, the authority of what they said was indisputable. It gave rise to a great freedom and simplicity of expression throughout the assembly, regardless of social or ecclesial position. It marked people spiritually and remains a point of reference in the world of the French Church. The voice of the poor was revealed as a true authority: a voice which comes from an experience of living through great trials. It sounds like a call which comes from a place beyond the hardest challenges and which still resounds with long-endured suffering and struggle.

Those who spoke at Lourdes forced us to look beyond their own experience, to those who are poorer than they are. Knowing themselves to be precarious, they nonetheless invited us to turn our gaze to people beyond them, meaning that everyone, including themselves, are invited to experience God's 'Preferential Option for the Poor'. This exercise does not define a group we can refer to and then stop looking. This Option for the poor presents itself, through experience, as a dynamic movement guided by people in poverty themselves, which takes each and every person together and leads them to those who are even more marginalized, to those who are becoming completely invisible. The authority with which people like these speak does not come from belonging to this or that particular group: it is the authority of those who are missing, who are absent from our common humanity, because we no longer see them. Everyone can observe this fact if they go out to meet these people, guided by those living in close contact with them, their brothers and sisters in poverty. This authority is audible, although it is not yet fully manifested. It is not dependent on a particular experience which would make it standard and pretend to tell the truth on its own. It is experienced alongside the people who are living it. This point is essential for churches to understand if they wish to take the context of contemporary democratic values seriously.

An objection could arise: the words of these people living in poverty have been developed in a working group, they are not their own! The speech from which we quoted an extract owes much to those working alongside the group, those who do not belong to the world of poverty and who facilitated the implementation of the project. Who speaks in this work? If it is not speech made directly by people in extreme poverty, it is still a speech born of true dialogue, part of an exchange, a listening exercise. The text is the result of an engagement through which people without a voice were able to speak of the reality of their situation with the whole of their being. Is there ever a possibility for any of us of accessing that which is 'voiceless' within us, without using such methods of interaction and engagement? These methods were used in order to enable others to adapt their stories to a different environment from their own. The word which was spoken was then able to match the experience articulated by the person who told their story. The speeches were only able to be given life in the context of a relationship of trust in the leaders and the tradition which feeds them – the movement ATD Fourth World and the Christian faith.

II The lesson the Church can learn from people in precarious circumstances

Once they have recognized the authority of the voices of poor people, Churches still have to learn how to take on board and use what these same people are saying to change their message. We will give only three examples here, through the lenses of human relationships, hope and history.

The first lesson is linked to human relationships. Meeting people in great poverty requires us to abandon reference to the frameworks through which we build and organize the world: frameworks which constantly force us to work at classifying, evaluating, prioritizing, controlling, etc. It is not possible to participate in societal interaction without putting these frameworks into practice, which allow us to adjust to proposals and check the points of agreement and disagreement. But, when brought face to face with those who are poor, these filters lose their usual invisibility, make us feel the weight of their claims, and reveal the way they are distorted. Alongside those who suffer, we are led to experience something simpler: the experience of being welcomed 'just because you are you', without any other reason. Those who are usually considered unimportant force those who meet them to change their approach: as soon as the relationship becomes one of exchange for the benefit of the other, the vulnerable person flees, sensing that that is what it is.

People on the margins of society constantly lead us to the most precious core of human relationships, this ability we have to communicate with one another, to give one another new life when we say to them once again that we care about them. The need to progress up the ladder of society dissolves. An encounter with those who are poor requires us to rediscover that which gives us life, primarily a friendship, a 'because you are you'. This echoes the phrase which God says every day to humanity: 'because you are my people'. This phrase is a relationship which calls us back to our origins, which creates an unbreakable bond, and which, paradoxically, frees us, because it is simply a call to be born. Even monetary exchanges – a major feature of the global economy – thoroughly characterized by force and control, could not hold up for one minute if they too were not based on the ability to communicate with others as potential partners, respondents, living beings. This gracious feature, visible even in these kinds of relationships, means that the economy – which

60

may be regarded as a false God which only knows how to organize competition with no care for the loser – is able to play a completely different role provided it does not leave its dark side unchecked. Those whom we have habitually ignored have the ability to bring a beating heart into the centre of our exchanges. An encounter with the most vulnerable reveals that, although love is mixed with other desires, it is nevertheless still present.

A second space for learning concerns hope. People living in poverty often have this right to their core. More often than not, their childhood scarred them deeply. It is as if, from the very beginning, their existence was taken hostage by one type of violence or another: neglect, abuse, exploitation, insecurity. It is as if the first gift of life (that which makes us human) was attacked at the root, leaving very little opportunity to recognize and talk about it.

This life which has been so painfully experienced continues nonetheless to be permeated by a strong sense of principle. This remains an object of wonder. Is this a sign that being in the world carries within itself a promise which abides despite the injuries which occurred even at birth? The suffering or rebellion of the poor attests to this: just by being alive we can hear the call which we all desire to follow. People who are put back together after a disastrous start in life have been able to associate this promise with the commitment and care of those who helped them to carry on living. With that as a starting point, they have been able to trust in the promise and, in turn, rely on it. The others, those who must fend for themselves, remain severely bruised, hampered in their movements by the conditions of their arrival in the world. However, very few of them give up. Even if they had to mourn the lack of any chance of success, they keep hold of a faint promise in their heart, a call just to them, and this is an indication of where the secret of their hope lies.

The presence of people who are marked by extreme poverty, with all the struggles that entails, forces us to notice the precariousness of life. It teaches us to read history in a new way. It recalls that existence is far more than a kind of linear progress fuelled by our own success: it is a hazardous journey, marked by numerous falls, but also by the strength to rise again. The concept of 'rhythm', developed by Henri Maldiney and used by Philippe Charru, helps us to understand this path of highs and lows. Rhythm is what responds to the experience of vertigo, when we lose all our bearings, when our environment becomes chaotic and we feel we are under threat of being overwhelmed.

The rhythm establishes a base from which recovery can take place and living space open up. This process of being knocked down and getting back up again can be regarded as the fundamental anthropological fact of a life which is marked by a kind of deep pulse. In all human endeavour, the trace of this primal experience of fall and recovery can be felt. It is a given: our life, the history of mankind, is a constant struggle to get back on our feet again. It seems this is the most beautiful thing – and the saddest thing – about our existence.

When we no longer listen to the deep pulse, rhythms become cadences. We are no longer comfortable in our most basic experience. The regular beats no longer lead us to embrace the game of life again and again, but simply to an obligation to repeat the same movements together at the same time. If humanity continues to advance, it loses contact with its life-giving centre, with its experience of a struggle and getting back up. It behaves like an automaton. As this kind of rhythm only feeds on itself, it accelerates. It goes faster and faster and moves further and further away from what formed its essential core. It confuses the agitation of the race with the embracing of life.

The presence of people who are poor forces us to remember that there can be no human existence without help from others, the giving and receiving of support. Walking alongside the most vulnerable invites us to rediscover the human adventure as shared faith. It brings to the fore our responsibility for mutually supporting each other and the energy gained from that support. Our lives are then no longer a crazy race, but an experience of ups and downs, communicating with and using infinite variations on rhythms which become more complex but do not descend into chaos.

III   Rethinking church with those who are left aside

Shouldn't our understanding of church be reconsidered when we come into contact with people who are marginalized? We automatically define the Church as the community of believers, who have a message – the good news – to share with the world. A meeting like Diaconia 2013 shows that the faith of those present is invigorated by those who do not dare enter a church. (Very often people who experience poverty do not feel comfortable in churches. Rightly or wrongly, they feel they are being judged and misunderstood.) Let's re-read the Gospels in order to discover the vital role played by people in great distress.

Among these people, two figures emerge: the petitioners and the possessed. Overwhelmed by their distress or that of someone close to them, the first group come to Jesus with a gesture or a cry out to the one they believe can save them. According to the Synoptic Gospels, Jesus welcomes and often praises their trust: 'Your faith has saved you.' Maybe their faith saves them because they give themselves without holding back and with plenty of hope. Who, apart from these people pushed to the extremities, can live such a relationship with Christ? That is why he lets himself express admiration (Matt. 8.10). Another particularly important figure in distress is that of the possessed person, imprisoned and isolated (the demons make them deaf and dumb). The Gerasene demoniac, for example, lives in the tombs with the dead (Mark 5.1–20). Jesus never criticizes the possessed for their situation. He speaks to them and so delicately separates them from that which prevents them from living. Although this diptych does not summarize all forms of evil, the faces of the pleading and the possessed summarize nevertheless the two main situations of great distress, like a great dividing line offering few other possibilities outside of it.

How does the community of disciples formed around Jesus react to these meetings? This group enables the spread of the good news and places it in a specific time period. It shares the memory of Christ and allows us access to the time he lived in. In the Gospels, the disciples are often described as 'slow to believe' and reluctant to grant the requests of the petitioners. At best they say nothing, and sometimes they become annoyed: 'send her away, for she keeps crying after us' (Matt. 15.23). Jesus allows meetings between the disciples and people in distress who are 'pleading' or 'possessed'. Through this confrontation, he saves both from their possible imprisonment. The disciples need to learn faith from those in need and to shake themselves out of the temptation to shut themselves off with Jesus in a comfortable and exclusive relationship: 'send the people away' (Mark 6.36). The petitioners, for their part, need the disciples, so as not to retreat into the single-mindedness of their plea – even more important for the possessed. The presence of the disciples notes their supplication and actions. Because of them, their cry gives rise to a story.

Does this rapid return to the gospel and the experience of Diaconia 2013 not invite the Church to imagine itself as bigger than just the congregation of believers? Is it not in this place that disciples and people in distress – petitioner or possessed – can find Christ? Understood in this way, the Church is above all a reminder of the bestowal of salvation. The spiritual core of every one of us is found in connection with others, beginning with those who are usually left out of social interactions. In this meeting, God makes himself known.

For churches, this is a different way to be involved in public life. Rather than jumping first to defend our points of view, we can allow ourselves instead to be disturbed by outsiders: those who are usually ignored. By exposing ourselves to that which the gospel invites us to do, we as churches can speak, act and give of ourselves. In this way, we are able to contribute to the common good in a way which is both vigorous and just. By this type of approach and attitude, it is possible for us to begin to sketch out a challenge to globalization, which can be received by all people, which is broader and more inspiring than just speaking out in order to denounce it. It can show in a positive way that there are alternative paths other than those of competition and the elimination of those who are less profitable to society. Even more importantly, it can show that these very same people are the ones who have the ability to awaken in all a desire to live in community.

The Poor after Liberation Theology

JUNG MO SUNG

In Evangelii gaudium *Pope Francis says that we live in a world marked by exclusion, social inequality and the globalization of indifference in the face of these grave social problems. He places these problems at the centre of theological reflection and evangelization by saying that this culture is a product of the 'idolatry of money', a new version of the adoration of the golden calf. This article shows how this theological critique came to birth within liberation theology and the importance of a theological critique of economics as a path to living a non-idolatrous faith.*

The editors asked me to write about 'The poor after liberation theology', tackling contemporary 'post-liberationist' discourses about poverty and the Church of the Poor. The phrase 'after liberation theology' (LT) caught my attention as soon as I started to think about the article. 'After LT' can be understood in two senses. The first is 'theological discourses about the poor after the end of LT'. The second is 'think about the relationship between the poor and theology/the Church after what LT said'. In the second sense, LT is seen as a watershed or an important point in the discussion about the poor, poverty and theology/the Church.

It is not possible to discuss the present state of LT in this article, so I will take for granted the second sense of 'after LT' and present some LT contributions to contemporary Church discussion of poverty, particularly in the document *Evangelii gaudium*.

I   *Evangelii gaudium* and idolatry

In discussing the context in which we proclaim the gospel, Pope Francis says: 'Just as the commandment "Thou shalt not kill" sets a clear limit in order to safeguard the value of human life, today we also have to say "thou shalt not" to an economy of exclusion and inequality. Such an economy kills' (EG 53). For an idea of the scale of social inequality in the world, the 85 richest people possess the equivalent of the total wealth of 46 per cent of the world's population.

This statement places at the centre of the Church's mission the challenge of exclusion and social inequality, which is the understanding of poverty in terms of two relationships: (a) in the perspective or inclusion in or exclusion from the market, the poor cease to be exploited in order to be excluded as 'leftovers' or 'surplus' (EG 53); (b) in the perspective of society as a whole, poverty is seen within the huge social inequality between rich and poor.

After this economic and social critique the Pope introduces a cultural and ethical perspective and says that to maintain the selfish ideal of a luxurious life-style that produces exclusion it has been necessary to develop a 'globalization of indifference' (EG 54). The idea of a globalization of indifference in the face of the sufferings of so many millions of excluded and poor people faces us with a question: has the human race lost the ability to feel compassion? Neuro-scientists tell us that empathy is a characteristic of the human species, part of the very process of learning and social interaction. Our current indifference is thus a cultural product capable of neutralizing the biological process of empathy, which would lead us to compassion. In the words of Boaventura de Souza Santos, one of the leading intellectuals of the World Social Forum, 'We are living at a time in which the most shocking social injustices seem incapable of generating the moral indignation and political will necessary to combat them effectively and to create a more just and decent society.'[1]

This fascination for consumerism and indifference to evil and the suffering of others seems to demand an explanation that touches a deeper dimension of the human being and life in society. The Pope goes beyond moral and cultural explanations and points to the theological dimension of this great social challenge. He says that this culture of indifference is a product of the 'idolatry of money' and that 'the worship of the ancient golden calf (cf. Exod. 32.1–35) has returned in a new and ruthless guise in the idolatry of money and the dictatorship of an impersonal economy lacking a truly human purpose' (EG 55).

With this statement, the challenge of poverty in its current form of exclusion and huge social inequality ceases to be a chapter of social teaching and becomes a central question for evangelization and theology.

We are not proclaiming God to an atheist world, but to an idolatrous world, a world which treats money as an absolute and inhibits the moral indignation and political will to fight the injustices and deaths suffered by the weakest. If this is so, theology has the task of unmasking the idol that supports this economy of exclusion and culture of indifference. With the idea of the 'idolatry of money', the Pope is calling on us to think about the relationship between idolatry, a fundamental theme in the Bible, and the fetish money. In other words, to make a theological critique of economics.

This way of seeing the relationship between evangelization and the challenge of poverty, between theology and economics, is not very common in theological or Church circles. Where does this perspective come from? Without claiming to exhaust the topic, my hypothesis is that it came from liberation theology or is at least heavily influenced by it. That is, this way of seeing the relationship between poverty, theology and the Church's mission grew up 'after' LT's contributions.

II   Moral indignation and non-idolatrous faith

From the beginning of LT, at the end of the 1960s and beginning of the 1970s, the principal liberation theologians have always insisted that LT is a second stage. The first stage is the activity of the poor to achieve liberation, which arises out of moral indignation at the huge scale of poverty in Latin America. In this sense, moral indignation is the zero moment that defines LT as a theology directed towards the transformation of the human and social relations that produce this indignation.

Indignation is part of the human condition. We are not creatures that react only to stimuli of pleasure and pain, but also to what we regard as immoral or contrary to fundamental values of the culture in which we live. In the face of situations that we regard as normal or compatible with our fundamental values, we do not get angry; we are indifferent or in favour. What the Pope is criticizing is this indifference of the world towards exclusion and social inequality. The excluded are seen as 'non-persons' and their sufferings are unimportant. In this vision of the world, social indignation flares up when the excluded burst into society fighting for their rights.

What produced the movement that was to lead to Latin American LT was the feeling of moral indignation of groups of Christians at massive poverty, at a social situation unworthy of human beings, a situation that denied the dignity of these poor people. This moral indignation burst out and broke with the prevailing moral, cultural and religious values. It was the experience of seeing the dignity of these people behind the label 'poor', worthless, applied to them by the dominant culture. Liberation theology understood this as the spiritual experience of seeing the face of Jesus in the face of the poor.

The battles on behalf of the poor that followed this experience did not have as their ultimate aim economic, social or political transformation, but the assertion 'of their human dignity and their status as daughters and sons of God'.[2] Transforming society was a means to enable all people, including the poor, to live a life worthy of their dignity as human beings. It wasn't a battle to enable the poor to imitate the luxurious lives of those well integrated into the market, but for the construction of a social system in which everyone is respected and in which everyone can live decently.

People who joined the struggle as a result of this spiritual experience realized that there was an incoherence between their faith and struggle experiences and the theologies they had learned. These theologies paid little or no attention to these issues – they were indifferent to them – and, worse, some of them presented this situation as the will of God. In this way questions arose about the relation between the experience of faith in the struggle and the dominant religious and theological languages in the Church. There is a text of Hugo Assmann's, from right at the beginning of LT, which expresses this problem and the challenge very well: 'If the historical situation of dependence and domination suffered by two-thirds of humanity, with its 30 million deaths a year from hunger and malnutrition, does not become the starting point for any Christian theology today, even in the rich and dominant countries, theology will be unable to situate and identify historically its fundamental themes. Its questions will not be real questions. They will make no contact with real men and women. That meant, as a participant of the Buenos Aires meeting remarked, that "theology has to be saved from its cynicism". Because really, in the face of the problems of today's world, many theological texts sink to the level of cynicism.'[3]

In this sense, one of the characteristics of LT is to assert that a theology of liberation is not possible without a liberation of theology. Christian faith and theologies that are indifferent to the suffering of a sister or brother are no more than forms of idolatry. This is why Gustavo Gutiérrez, in his classic book *A Theology of Liberation*, says: 'Theology as critical reflection thus fulfils a liberating function for man and the Christian community, preserving them from fetishism and idolatry.'[4] Compassion in the face of the suffering of the poor and excluded thus becomes a criterion for identifying a non-idolatrous faith.[5]

III   Dependency and liberation

A theology that sees itself as critical reflection on following the path of Jesus as embodied in the struggles to ensure that everyone can have a decent life necessarily comes up against the questions about the causes of this poverty and how it can be overcome. This produces an awareness that philosophy, which for so many centuries was the preferred dialogue partner of theology, is no longer sufficient. Without a hypothesis about the causes of mass poverty and the indifference of society and the state to the suffering of the poor, it is not possible to proclaim good news for a particular historical context or join in battles for transformation.

For this reason, from the very beginning, LT started a dialogue with the social sciences. At this time the dominant ideology in Latin American countries was the myth of developmentalism. Poverty was viewed as the product of underdevelopment and the way to overcome it was to follow the path previously mapped out by the rich industrialized countries. History was seen in a linear perspective: the poor underdeveloped countries should follow the path of industrialization taken by the rich countries and, for this purpose, open their doors to multinational companies that would take them on the road to development. It was assumed that there was no conflict of interest between the developed and underdeveloped countries.

In response to this theory a school of thought emerged in Latin America that has come to be known as 'dependency theory'. According to this, the development path would not solve the Latin American countries' social problems, including poverty, because these countries were dependent on the countries that occupied the centre of international capitalism. There was a conflict of interest, it was argued, between the peripheral countries and those at the centre of capitalism, and this relationship of dependency and economic exploitation would not allow the peripheral countries to develop. If development was possible within this relationship of dependency, it would be a dependent economic development with social dualism (a great separation between rich and poor), which is what in fact happened, for example, in Brazil.

The path advocated by dependency theory was that of autonomous development, freed from relationships of dependency. The liberation theologians adopted this dependency theory, with the introduction of other categories such as that of social classes, as their main instrument of analysis and understanding of society. The very term 'liberation' was conceived in relation to the idea of dependency. This is why Gustavo Gutiérrez says that the great task of that time was the construction of a society qualitatively different from the current one, based on new relations of production, in an attempt to put an end to the subjection of the poor, social classes and people to each other. For all these reasons, said Gutiérrez, 'To speak about the process of liberation begins to appear more appropriate and richer in human content.'[6]

Insofar as the idea of liberation is linked to a social analysis, it has a specific 'content' and recognizes the limits of historical possibilities. As a result, the aim is the construction of new relations of production – at that time called 'socialism' – with all the contradictions and limits this implies, to ensure that everyone should have their dignity and right to a decent life guaranteed.

In parallel to this more specific and historical idea of liberation, within LT an idea emerged of liberation 'conceived of as the overcoming of all enslavement' and 'as the vocation to be new men, creators of a new world'.[7] This extremely broad and abstract idea of 'the overcoming of all enslavement' has the advantage of being able to include all struggles and to attract more people with its 'promise', but it has the disadvantage of creating an expectation that is impossible to be met within human history and not being useful as a criterion for evaluating the results of particular struggles. For example, despite all the advances we have made in reducing social inequality in many countries of Latin America, confronted with the expectation of the end of all forms of slavery, the social improvements do not look like achievements or 'liberation', and we are left merely with a sense of failure or defeat.

Because of the limits of space in this article, it is not possible to go further into this question of the decline, from the 1990s onwards, of the close and critical dialogue with the social sciences on the part of some of the best known LT authors, but it is important to insist that this type of theological production has not disappeared from Latin American theology. The problem is that for commercial reasons these works are not published in languages other than Portuguese or Spanish and are not widely known.[8]

IV   Idolatry and capitalism as religion

The struggle inspired by the moral indignation we discussed earlier gave rise to a third question: how is it possible for capitalist societies to grow and fascinate wide sectors of the population while at the same time condemning so many people to exclusion and poverty? How is it that these social problems do not produce problems of conscience that act as a brake on the expansion of capitalism in the world? This is a much wider question than the indifference of theology to poverty; it is about the deep root of the indifference of the population in capitalist societies.

Right at the beginning of LT, Hugo Assmann, in dialogue with Marx's thought, the critical theory of the Frankfurt School and Lévi-Strauss, tried to expose the religious myths and symbols underlying capitalism in order to explain the fascination it exercised, despite its sacrificial nature in condemning millions to poverty and death. He said: 'The right succeeds in playing with popular myths whose roots are hidden. Since fetishism is the essence of this materialized religion ... that is capitalism, it should not surprise us that the right should be expert in fetishizing reality.' As early as the beginning of the 1970s, Assmann analysed capitalism as a religion: 'The most perfect "religion" has appeared, capitalism. In it religious perversion reaches perfection because religion itself has become entirely a commodity and a consumer product.'[9] On the basis of this theological analysis of capitalism, Assmann foresaw the globalization of fetishism and indifference and presented a serious challenge to theology: 'Capitalism is continuing to refine its materialist religious inversion; the fetishization of everything is the inevitable destiny of capitalism. Consequently the analysis of its methods of domination also continues to want and demand a terminology that will penetrate the symbolic, mythic and religious universe.'[10]

Fetishism is the inversion of the subject–object relationship: the human being becomes the object of the object produced by the human being who becomes the subject of the relationship. In the money and commodity fetish the 'value' of people is measured by their capacity to produce luxury goods. This results in the obsession with consumption and the unlimited accumulation of wealth – to become infinite – while the poor are seen as non-persons.

Moving in the same direction, in 1980 a book was published that is fundamental for the history of LT, *Gods in Struggle: The Idols of Oppression and the Search for the Liberating God.* In the introduction to the book, produced by the 'DEI team' (the Ecumenical Research Department of San José, Costa Rica), we read: 'In Latin America today the central problem is not the question of atheism, the ontological problem of the existence or not of God... The central problem lies in idolatry, the worship of the false gods of the system of oppression. More tragic than atheism is the problem of faith and hope in the false gods of the system. Every system of oppression has just this feature: it creates gods and produces idols that consecrate anti-life oppression... The search for the true God in this struggle among the gods leads us to anti-idolatrous discernment of false gods, of the fetishes that kill and their deadly religious weapons.... We believe that the problem of the idols of oppression and the search for the liberating God today acquires a new dimension, both in the work of evangelization and in political work. This is where liberation theology meets one of its most fruitful challenges.'[11]

Idols are gods that demand sacrifices of human lives. Therefore those who kill in the name of their idol-god have no problems of conscience, still less for the victims of the sacrifice. In 1989, Hugo Assmann and Franz Hinkelammert published another book that is fundamental to this critique, *Idolatry of the Market: An Essay on Economics and Theology.*[12] In this book, they showed that in economic theories and processes there is a strange metamorphosis of the gods. And, with neoliberalism, the free market is raised to the category of the absolute and the laws of the market become the ultimate criterion for the organization of social and economic life and the foundation of the demands for the sacrifice of the lives of the poor and for indifference in the face of exclusion and social inequality. These authors do not reduce theology to scientific economics. What they do is reveal the 'endogenous' theology that moves capitalism. In this sense, it is a development of the intuitions already present, as we saw above, at the beginning of liberation theology.

And at the beginning of the 1990s, after the great changes in the world, the rise of neoliberalism, economic globalization and the fall of the socialist bloc, Assmann and other liberation theologians insisted that the main issue of the period – which continues today, according to Pope

Francis – was social exclusion and social insensitivity to that exclusion.

From the beginning of LT, Assmann, Gutiérrez, Franz Hinkelammert, Pablo Richard and others stressed the idolatrous religious dimension of capitalism, anticipating the debate that would take place among social scientists after the publication of a previously unknown text of Walter Benjamin's 'Capitalism as Religion'.[13] In criticizing capitalism as being or having an idolatrous religious structure, LT and the Pope are redefining the relationship between modernity and evangelization. The mission of the Church is not to proclaim God to the world that no longer believes in God's existence, but to proclaim the God of Life, who opts for the poor in order to demonstrate the dignity of all, in a world marked by the idolatry of money. And in this task I think that LT still has much to contribute.

V   Closing remarks

To end this article I want to go back to the initial idea of LT, that the 'zero' moment is moral indignation and the spiritual experience of finding the face of Jesus in the face of the poor. The social struggles and the theological critiques of idolatry in the Church and in capitalism have as their ultimate aim the affirmation of the dignity of the poor and excluded and their right to a decent life.

On this path the poor affirm their dignity for themselves and society in struggles for a more just society and by taking part in the community life of the churches that open up to them. Opening the Church to the poor, being a Church of the Poor, is to give public witness that God is no respecter of persons, to affirm the dignity of the poor and to live a non-idolatrous faith. And the public affirmation of this dignity is a necessary condition for more people to become angry at the situation of the poor and for their sufferings to become a priority for society, with more political will and energy to bring about the necessary transformations.

Translated by Francis McDonagh

Notes

1. Boaventura de Souza Santos, *Se Deus fosse um activista dos direitos humanos*, Coimbra, 2013, p. 8.
2. Gustavo Gutiérrez, *We Drink from our Own Wells*, 2nd edn, Maryknoll, NY, 1984, and London, 1985, p. 1.

3. Hugo Assmann, *Teología desde la praxis de la liberación: ensayo teológico desde la América dependiente*, 2nd edn, Salamanca, 1976. (1st edn, 1973), p. 40.

4. Gustavo Gutiérrez, *A Theology of Liberation*, Maryknoll NY, 1973 and London, 1974, p. 12.

5. *Cf* Assmann, *Crítica à lógica da exclusão: ensaios sobre economia e teologia*, São Paulo, 1994, p. 14.

6. Gutiérrez, *A Theology of Liberation*, p. 27.

7. Leonardo Boff, *Teologia do cativeiro e da libertação*, Petrópolis, 2nd edn, 1980. (1st edn, Lisbon, 1976), p. 19.

8. For example, Franz Hinkelammert, *A maldição que pesa sobre a lei: as raízes do pensamento crítico em Paulo de Tarso*, São Paulo, 2012; Hugo Assmann and Jung Mo Sung, *Deus em nós: o reinado que acontece no amor solidário aos pobres*, São Paulo, 2012; Néstor Míguez, *Jesús del pueblo: para una cristología narrativa*, Buenos Aires, 2011.

9. Assmann, *Teología desde la práxis de liberación*, pp. 179 and 192.

10. Assmann, *Teología desde la práxis de liberación*, p. 183.

11. Various, *A luta dos deuses: os ídolos da opressão e a busca do Deus libertador*, São Paulo, 1982, pp. 7–8 (1st edn *La lucha de los dioses: los ídolos de la opresión y la búsqueda del Dios liberador*, San José, 1980).

12. Hugo Assmann and Franz Hinkelammert, *A idolatria do mercado: ensaio sobre economia e teologia*, Petrópolis, 1989.

13. Walter Benjamin, 'Kapitalismus als Religion [Fragment]', *Gesammelte Schriften* VI, Frankfurt am Main, 1991, pp. 100–3.

74

Part Two: Poverty and Resistance in Global Contexts

Migrants and the Church in the Age of Globalization: An Asian Perspective

GEMMA TULUD CRUZ

Human mobility has always been a part of Asia's story. The age of globalization, however, has contributed to massive movements of Asians whose experience presents a rich and compelling locus for theological consideration. This essay explores the experience of vulnerable migrants in Asia, particularly the unskilled workers, and the Asian Church's response to their plight. The essay argues that the Church becomes a true Church of the Poor in the context of migration when words are complemented by deeds and the mission for transformation is shared with/by migrants themselves.

I Migration in Asia in the age of globalization

Asia has a long history of permanent, temporary and cyclical migration due to trade, labour, religion or cultural interchange. In pre-colonial times, the Malay peninsula and the Indonesian and Philippine archipelagos was an area marked by mobility of people of various ethnicities, especially via the sea. Colonization, however, intensified the movement of Asian peoples. First, territorial conquests and regulation of trade by European colonial regimes forced the migration of Asians as indentured labourers. From 1834 to 1937 alone, some 30 million men and women from the Indian subcontinent were brought to Southeast Asia, Africa, the Caribbean and the Pacific to work in British plantations.[1] The two world wars also propelled significant migration among Asians as the colonizers used or recruited many of their former subjects to be foot soldiers in the war, then lured more by opening their doors to immigrants to help rebuild war-devastated economies. Three major political events, in the meantime, triggered massive migration among Asians from the 1970s well into the 1990s. The West–East Pakistan conflict forcibly displaced around ten million people, while the war in Vietnam, which spilled into Laos and Cambodia, saw the exodus of about three million people from the region. Last but not the least, the successive waves of occupation and political crises in Afghanistan – from the Russians to the Taliban – have led to the displacement of millions of people in 71 different countries.

Modern transport and communication technologies, continuing political and economic crises, environmental disasters and wars and religio-cultural conflicts in many Asian countries, as well as real or fabricated stories of better life in the destination countries, displaced or encouraged many more Asians to migrate – both documented and undocumented – from the 1990s onwards. Since the 1990s, however, Asian migration remarkably changed largely due to the effects of globalization. First, Asian migration considerably changed in terms of volume. A UN report, for example, states that in 2013 Asians represented the largest diaspora group residing outside their major area of birth, accounting for about 19 million migrants living in Europe, some 16 million in Northern America and about three million in Oceania. The same report provides evidence of another significant change among Asians on the move, that is, Asians are moving overwhelmingly in search of work. The report indicates that compared to other regions of destination, Asia saw the largest increase of international migrants since 2000, adding some 20 million migrants in 13 years, and that this growth was mainly fuelled by the increasing demand for foreign labour in the oil-producing countries of Western Asia and in South-Eastern Asian countries with rapidly growing economies, such as Malaysia, Singapore and Thailand.[2] In 2012, for example, more than one million Filipinos left the country to work in a country of the Gulf Cooperation Council (GCC), in Singapore, or in Hong Kong. More than 250,000 workers from Sri Lanka and 100,000 from Thailand have also been leaving their country every year since 2008.[3] Such information gives credence to a new trend in global migration in general, and Asian migration in particular, that is, that South–South migration is as common as South–North migration.

II   The plight of unskilled migrants in Asia

In keeping with the trajectories of international labour migration, particularly as created by the current process of economic globalization, the majority of the Asian migrant workforce is undeniably unskilled and move on a temporary basis from less developed to industrializing countries. These unskilled workers and, in particular, the undocumented unskilled workers, constitute the underclass among Asian migrants for a couple of reasons. First of all, they bore the brunt of the three dominant and problematic attitudes towards migrants in key destination countries in Asia: (1) immigrants should not be allowed to settle; (2) foreign residents should not be offered citizenship except in exceptional cases; and (3) national culture and identity should not be modified in response to external influences.[4] As a result there are thousands of stateless children of migrants, especially unskilled and undocumented workers, in countries such as South Korea, Saudi Arabia and Japan.

These problematic attitudes towards migrants are exacerbated by unjust working conditions[5] as well as restrictive and exploitative immigration policies towards unskilled workers, which force those who are documented to go undocumented. Taiwan's undocumented migration, for example, increased starting in the late 1980s due to the limitation to a non-renewable three-year contract, which forces people to return to Taiwan with forged documents while others run away from their exploitative jobs and, consequently, become undocumented workers. Hong Kong's case is more problematic, primarily because it only gave laid off workers two weeks to find new work or else be deported. This was insufficient, particularly for foreign domestic workers, who are often pushed to an undocumented situation. In the Middle East, meanwhile, migrant workers are able to enter only through sponsorship by *khafel*[6] and are required to surrender their passports to the *khafel* as soon as they enter the country. The *khafel* must give clearance before the worker can leave the country. In addition, workers are prohibited from changing employers and, therefore, are literally at the mercy of the sponsors. Turning to undocumented employment then often becomes a means of escaping from a situation of bondage, thereby creating an underclass within the underclass, that is, the undocumented unskilled worker.

III   The Asian Church's response to migration

The Church in Asia recognizes the immense and complex difficulties and challenges that confront migrants in Asia, particularly vulnerable groups such as unskilled and undocumented workers who embody the poor among Asian migrants by virtue of the stronger discrimination and exploitation they experience. As such the Asian Church responds in two ways. The first is through moral guidance and vision. Even when the Federation of Asian Bishops (FABC) has not yet issued formal statements on migration, for example, the bishops of the Philippines (1988) and Taiwan (1989) released their own statements on migration. It was in its Final Statement for its Fifth Plenary Assembly (1990) that the FABC made a clear link for the first time between poverty and migration by pointing at how poverty 'drives both men and women to become migrant workers, often destroying family life in the process' (2.2.1).[7] In 1993, the Korean Church also addressed the issue of undocumented migrants and their problems through a statement of the Justice and Peace Committee which emphasized the need to look at the issue from a human rights perspective and to go beyond a national approach to embrace a 'mature citizens' consciousness and conscious solidarity with the global family'.[8] Moreover, subsequent plenary assemblies of the FABC after its Fifth Plenary Assembly included discussions or references to migration urging special attention to the displaced, e.g. political and ecological refugees and migrant workers. FABC VI, for example, exhorts the faithful to welcome these marginalized and exploited people for 'in welcoming them we expose the cause of their displacement, work toward conditions for a more humane living in community, experience the universal dimension of the Kingdom (Gal. 3.28) and appreciate new opportunities for evangelization and intercultural dialogue'.[9] These statements are complemented by initiatives such as the FABC Office for Human Development's symposium on Filipino migrant workers in Asia and the Faith Encounters in Social Action's (FEISA) fifth gathering entitled 'From Distrust to Respect ... Reject to Welcome: Study Days on Undocumented Migrants and Refugees'.[10]

The Asian Church also responds to the plight of migrants through advocacy and moral action. The Church in Asia recognizes the fact that discussions and analyses of the plight of migrants are not enough. FABC believes that migration and refugee movements challenge the Asian Church to 'evolve life-giving, service-oriented programs of action within the pastoral mission of the Church' (FABC VII, art. 5).[11] Hence, FABC's 'Colloquium on the Church in Asia in the Twenty-First Century', held in Thailand in 1997, even urged dioceses to 'more actively take up the cause of migrant workers through the legal process of the host country by providing financial support and lawyers to fight for their rights'.[12] To be sure, such exhortations have not fallen on deaf ears. My years of work on migration have brought me into close encounters with Asians (clergy and lay as well as migrants themselves) in Asia and around the world, where I have seen the manifold ways in which a Church of the Poor comes to life for and with migrants. I once participated, for example, at a pre-departure orientation session for Filipina domestic workers bound for the Middle East, where the religious sister running the workshop literally told the participants, especially those going to Saudi Arabia, not to bring religious articles such as the rosary or the Bible. There must have been a sense of discomfort for the sister to say it, but it is clear that the wellbeing of the migrant is the ultimate concern of the Church. A more detailed discussion on this topic is not possible here, but let me mention the Catholic Church of Hong Kong as a clear example.[13] The diocese of Hong Kong, which is faced with the challenge of caring for the thousands of migrant domestic workers, particularly from the Philippines, has its own pastoral centre for migrant Filipinos (it is open to other migrants). It also offers a variety of services from the more basic needs such as language classes, to the more urgent ones such as hotlines or legal assistance to those in distress and the more strategic ones such as livelihood and reintegration programs. The centre also provides much-needed space for gatherings where the migrant domestic workers not only attend to their needs but also to those of their fellow migrants and, to a certain extent, the local community, especially through their volunteer work. What is clear in all these initiatives is that the mission of the Church among migrants in Asia is a shared mission that is built on incarnational evangelization. It is not just owned and embraced by the clergy, religious and pastoral agents but also by the migrants themselves. Moreover, it is about witness as 'withness', about accompaniment. It is about a Church of the Poor where the poor – in this case, the migrants – are not simply passive recipients but also active agents in the transformation of their lives, the Church and the world.

Notes

1. Manolo Abella and Lin Lean Lim, 'The Movement of People in Asia: Internal, Intra-regional and International Migration', in Christian Conference of Asia, Uprooted People in Asia, Hong Kong, 1995, p. 12.
2. See '232 million international migrants living abroad worldwide – new UN global

migration statistics reveal', http://esa.un.org/unmigration/wallchart2013.htm.

3. Asian Development Bank Institute, *Labor Migration, Skills, and Student Mobility in Asia*, Tokyo: Asian Development Bank Institute, 2014, p. 4. The phenomenon of one million Filipinos leaving the country annually to be OFWs (Overseas Filipino Workers) has been happening since 2006. See Maruja Asis, 'Philippines', *Asian and Pacific Migration Journal* ,17.3–4 (2008), p. 367.

4. Stephen Castles, 'The Myth of the Controllability of Difference: Labor Migration, Transnational Communities and State Strategies in East Asia', http://www.unesco.org/most/apmrcast.htm.

5. Photographer Philippe Chancel, for example, describes migrant construction workers in the United Arab Emirates as 'the new slaves' of the Gulf. Tim Hume, 'Photographer captures "new slaves" of the Gulf', http://edition.cnn.com/2011/11/11/world/meast/emirates-workers-art/index.html.

6. The *khafel* system is a sponsorship system for recruitment, a form of franchise to import foreign labour granted to loyal subjects, which thrives on bringing in ever-increasing numbers of foreign workers willing to pay money for their jobs.

7. Gaudencio Rosales and Catalino Arevalo (eds), *For All The Peoples of Asia: Federation of Asian Bishops' Conferences Documents from 1970–1991*, New York, 1992, pp. 276–7.

8. As quoted in Graziano Battistella, 'The Poor in Motion: Reflections on Unauthorized Migration', *Asian Christian Review,* 4.2 (2010), p. 76.

9. Franz-Josef Eilers (ed.), *For All The Peoples of Asia Volume 2: Federation of Asian Bishops' Conferences Documents from 1992–1996*, Quezon City, 1997, p. 11.

10. For a more comprehensive treatment on FABC and migration, see Jonathan Tan, 'An Asian Theology of Migration', in Peter Phan and Elaine Padilla (eds), *Contemporary Issues of Migration and Theology*, New York, 2014, pp. 121–38.

11. Franz-Josef Eilers (ed.), *For All The Peoples of Asia Volume 3: Federation of Asian Bishops' Conferences Documents from 1997–2001*, Quezon City, 2002, p. 11. Hereafter referred to as *FAPA III*.

12. *FAPA III*, p. 40.

13. For examples on Protestant churches, see Judy Chan, 'Welcoming the Stranger: Christian Hospitality to Refugees and Asylum Seekers in Hong Kong', *CTC Bulletin,* XXVIII.1 (2012), pp. 41–61.

Urgent: The War on Drugs Has Failed

RONILSO PACHECO

This article discusses an extremely disturbing theme in Latin America: the limits of the War on Drugs policy as the main instrument of public policy in the region to solve the problem of production, consumption and trafficking of drugs, and how it leads to a trail of corruption, violence and criminalization of the poorest memebers of society. The article will seek to broaden the discussion of the topic, from a brief analysis of the problem to its complex repercussions in the context of a continent marked by poverty, inequality and popular resistance.

The Mexican anthropologist Salvador Maldonado Aranda has written: 'It is an urgent task to understand the drugs trade in terms of the changes in the state and neoliberalism brought about by globalization, and try to analyze the particular territories in which legal and illegal drugs are produced or processed and, subsequently, the ways in which the trade is being transnationalized.'[1]

In other words, when we look at the current situation of the drugs issue from the perspective of Latin America, it is increasingly difficult not to recognize the failure – and I would even say, the counter-productive lethality – of the War on Drugs policy, which is the principal strategy of the continent's governments. What is worse – and that is why this Mexican scholar's statement is so much needed – the War on Drugs policy has become, not only a militarized instrument of the 'legitimate use of force' in the poor neighbourhoods of the continent, but also an important instrument of geopolitical interference in international relations, used especially by the USA, which gives them free access to the territories of others (such as Brazil, Bolivia, Mexico and Colombia) on the grounds of self-defence against the 'drugs invasion' of their territories.

Nevertheless there is another important factor that makes the 'drugs war' policy an even more lethal strategy: its implementation over the decades has not succeeded in preventing the spread of violence and the exposure of society to the violence. The truth is that its main contribution is negative in two ways: (1) it is at the heart of the increase of violence, of which the main victims are the poorest,[2] and (2) it has produced a dizzying increase in the prison population in Latin America, notably in Brazil, which recently overtook Russia and rose to third place in the world rankings, with over 700,000 prisoners.

The War on Drugs policy also follows a very clear stigmatization script. This script is a sort of legacy of the authoritarian and unequal, steeply hierarchical society that was formed on our continent, well summed up by the Uruguayan author Eduardo Galeano in his classic *The Open Veins of Latin America*. This stigmatization takes the form of the construction of an 'objective profile' that might be of a social group whose relationship with drugs is seen as a threat, frightening and criminal; of particular territories in which the presence of drugs, either because they are produced there or because they circulate there, gives them an image of ungovernability, liable to arbitrary treatment and violence that take on the force of law; of physical bodies whose contact with drugs is summarily demonized and legitimates the repression imposed.

It is in this context that discourse comes to be used as power, in the strictest sense of Foucault's definition. Venezuelan author Rosa del Olmo had put this well: 'The important thing, therefore, seems not to be the substance or its definition, and still less its ability or not to alter a human being in some way, but the discourse that is constructed about it.'[3] Del Olmo talks about the various discourses constructed around drugs, one of which she describes as 'medico-penal'. Del Olmo's approach is shared by a number of Latin American scholars, especially those belonging to the school of so-called critical criminology.

From Argentina Brígida Rinoldi invoked Foucault to argue that 'Medicine has intervened for the purposes of controlling and modelling, creating a type of social organization based on classifications of individuals as "normal" and "pathological".'[4] And the Brazilian historian José Murilo de Carvalho, describing the marginalization of the poor of Rio de Janeiro at the end of the nineteenth century, says that when sanitary improvements were introduced, 'To avoid resistance from the residents, the [health] brigades asked armed police to accompany them.'[5] Police power comes in to back the authority of medical discourse. The Latin American War on Drugs policy is deeply marked by the continuation of the criminalization of poverty.

The growth of the drugs trade, which happily ignores any heavily armed repressive response and takes the majority of victims from both civil society and the 'troops' (those of the regular army and the drugs trade) who are involved in the direct confrontation, remains untouchable through its power to corrupt. The low pay of the security forces in most countries of the continent, compared with the easy money that circulates in great quantities in the drugs trade, makes it difficult to fight the real 'drug barons'. Soldiers and police are accused of using extreme force against petty dealers in poor neighbourhoods, but are easily bribed by the millions of dollars available to the bosses, who very often move freely among national elites and have 'contacts' in the police, political circles and even the judiciary.

I   The case of Colombia

For purposes of comparison, it is interesting to note how the Gospels show the region of Samaria as a place stigmatized and consequently criminalized by Jesus' Jewish contemporaries. In Luke, chapter 9, this stigma makes James and John ask Jesus to let them send fire from heaven on the Samaritans who would not let Jesus through their territory, and it is probably because of this reputation of the Samaritans among his audience that Jesus makes the Samaritan the hero of a story about the care of one's neighbour, whoever is vulnerable. In this case, from the place where they least expected it, solidarity came (and not from the priest or levite). The drugs trade and cocaine in Colombia have been the main factors in turning the country, thanks to US image-making, into a sort of 'Latin American Samaria'.

In the case of Colombia, dealing with the issue of drugs in isolation from any social context vitiates a broader understanding of a process that is much more complex than the cartels that became world famous in the 1980s and 1990s. Before it had anything to do with the cartels' power struggles, the growing sale and consumption of drugs has to do with the process of colonization and expansion of the frontier territories of the relevant states. Salvador Aranda again: 'It should be noted that the coca-producing regions, Caquetá and Putumayo, are also areas in which the processes of expansion of the Colombian state started with projects of territorial colonization and national integration.'[6]

It is therefore necessary to see the growth and expansion of the drugs trade also as a sort of by-product of the expansion of the neoliberal policies adopted by the governments of the countries concerned, such as Colombia. Since the beginning of the 1930s the political duel between conservatives and liberals has frustrated any possibility of any useful reform, such as those promised by President López Pumajero.[7] Even the so-called Bogotazo, sparked off by the assassination of the liberal leader Jorge Eliécer Gaitán in April 1948, led to one of the worst waves of violence Latin America has ever seen.

In the midst of all this intense conflict, the Colombian rural communities and the urban popular classes finally became frustrated by the signals of liberalization and freedom first made and then halted by the liberal and conservative oligarchies.[8] Such an impression was made by this conflict and this period that the subsequent generation was labelled the 'children of the Violence'.

The scene was one of poverty, political frustration and lack of prospects, especially in the rural areas. By the end of the 1970s and the beginning of the 1980s, Putumayo, Caquetá and Guaviare were territories of the most intensive cultivation of coca, not only in the region, but of the world. Also growing was the stereotype of the Latin American immigrant to the USA as the main channel for the entry of cocaine into the country, just as, in the American collective imagination, opium was associated with the Chinese at the beginning of the twentieth century and Mexicans with cannabis in the 1930s. At the beginning of the 1980s, Colombia was among the countries (alongside Mexico, Bolivia and others) targeted by the Gilman-Hawkins amendment approved by the US Congress, which suspended economic aid to countries that did not cooperate with the USA's anti-narcotics programme.[9] The War on Drugs policy was thus consolidated as the best discourse for North–South intervention.

In the midst of all this geopolitics at government level, when production in Putumayo was made illegal, the situation of the Colombian rural colonists became significantly worse. Illegality (or the criminalization of the territory) left the rural communities without employment and without any significant government support for agriculture. They were condemned to a clandestine existence, since survival demanded the continuance of cultivation, now in even more degrading and insecure conditions, while at the same time the drug traffickers demanded long days of work in precarious conditions and with payment sometimes made in drugs.[10]

One common feature of life for Colombians, Brazilians, Mexicans, Bolivians, Nicaraguans and other Latin Americans is a strong presence of churches and pastoral agencies in the poor neighbourhoods of all their cities across the continent. Protestants (in Brazil, especially Pentecostals) and Catholics seem in some way to 'subvert' both the hold of the drugs trade in the territories it tries to control and the presence and the operations of the police units responsible for crushing the trade. Churches are usually at the same time sites of resistance and shelters, a reinforcement of community identity and a 'moral refuge'. In territories constantly threatened by 'disorder', overshadowed by various forms of violence, become an *ou topos* space, the 'other space', the place in which violence does not dictate how to live and where security is not determined by the absence or presence of weapons.

II   A conclusion

At a general level, there are two points to think about. First, we need to insist on an analysis that encourages the deconstruction of the idea of the poor outskirts of our cities as random collections of poor people, lacking the presence of public social care. Instead, we need to see them as institutional forms, as the French anthropologist correctly defined the American ghettos he studied with such care. We have to expose the subtle tactics of the state, which keeps a mass of people under concealed control by making them pay for supposedly being a threat to our institutions and a source of social disorder.

Second, we need to insist on analysis of the power of language, which constructs identities and turns 'the other' into a caricature. Here attention needs to be focused on the media, television and print media especially. As the Brazilian sociologist Vera Malaguti has emphasized, the mass media are fundamental for the whole penal system to be able to exercise its power.[11] Fear and insecurity creates caricatures, faceless figures who tend to 'justify', as Malaguti puts it, 'the amputation of this collective being from the social body'. 'Unless your righteousness exceeds that of the scribes and Pharisees,...' It is wholly relevant to remember this advice of Jesus to his disciples in chapter 5 of Matthew's Gospel. Scribes and Pharisees are not unjust, but believe in the repressive and punitive system as a way of relieving social tensions and inequalities. It is like deterring adultery by stoning.

On his visit to Rio de Janeiro for World Youth Day, Pope Francis was, on the one hand, hard line as regards the legalization of drugs on the Uruguayan model, but on the other showed an understanding that 'we have to deal with the problems that are at the root of drug use'. The question of drugs does not involve a simple dispute between 'criminals' and 'victims', between 'healthy' and 'sick' users. Some thinking, therefore, must be done to allow us to move forward. Those who are inspired by love, justice and mercy must make a contribution that will allow us to have a policy on this continent that is both more humane and more effective.

Translated by Francis McDonagh

Notes

1. Alejo Vargas Velásquez (ed.), *Seguridad en democracia: Un reto a la violencia en América Latina*, Buenos Aires, 2010, www.clacso.org.ar/libreria-latinoamericana/buscar_libro_detalle.php?id_libro=495&campo=autor&texto=Vargas.
2. These are the majority of the approximately 50,000 violent deaths a year in Brazil, and civilians are the majority of the over 50,000 people killed by violence during the Calderón government in Mexico.
3. Rosa del Olmo, *A face oculta da droga*, Rio de Janeiro, 1990, p. 22 (original: *La cara oculta de la droga*, Bogotá, 1988).
4. Brígida Rinoldi, *Narcotráfico y Justicia en Argentina, la autoridad de lo escrito en el juicio oral*, Buenos Aires, 2008, p. 35.
5. José Murilo de Carvalho, *Os bestializados, o Rio de Janeiro e a república que não foi*, São Paulo, 1987, p. 94.
6. Alejo Vargas Velásquez (ed.), *Seguridad en democracia*, p. 355.
7. Ricardo Vélez Rodríguez, *Da guerra à pacificação, a escolha colombiana*, Campinas, SP, 2010, p. 25.
8. Rodríguez, *Da guerra à pacificação, a escolha colombiana*, p. 355.
9. del Olmo, *A face oculta da droga*, p. 62.
10. Velásquez, *Seguridad en democracia*, p. 357.
11. Vera Malaguti, *O medo na cidade do Rio de Janeiro, dois tempos de uma história*, Rio de Janeiro, 2003, p. 33.

Ecological and Ethical Implications of Pirating the Resources of Africa

PETER KANYANDAGO

The taking of the resources of other people without their consent, which I would like to call poroipiracy, *is almost as old as the history of humanity. However, systematic and justified* poroipiracy *involving people from different countries and continents can be said to be associated with Europe's spirit of discovery and conquest, which involved a violent plundering of resources and enslavement of peoples justified on religious grounds. Later,* poroipiracy *also involved nationals and the destruction of the environment and livelihoods of the affected people.*

The plundering of the resources of other people, *poroipiracy*,[1] is almost as old as the history of humanity. In its systematic and justified form, intercontinental *poroipiracy* is associated with Europe's two-pronged search for and taking of territories, and secondly of converting the non-Christians (pagans) to Christianity, especially beginning with the eleventh century. In most cases this went hand in hand with violence.[2] Such actions were originally justified on the religious grounds that pagans were seen to be the enemies of Christ and therefore did not merit owning and using their resources. In *poroipiracy* are included animate and inanimate things, such as mineral ores, land, forests and oil. This contribution would like to argue that *poroipiracy* leads to destruction of the environment and of livelihoods of the people concerned, as well as the dehumanization of the latter.

89

Peter Kantandago

I Religious and racial grounds for *poroipiracy*

The practice of taking others' resources is linked to a combination of historical, socio-economic, ethical and anthropological factors rooted in what has come to be known as the Doctrine (Right) of Discovery. A preliminary study by Tonya Gonella Frichner, rapporteur of the UN Special Forum on Indigenous Issues, gives a good background to this discussion.[3] The Doctrine of Discovery has gradually given rise to what can now be called international law or law of nations, especially in relation to 'discovering' and subduing indigenous people who were seen as infidels.[4] It is important to note for our discussion that this law was seen as the laws of Christendom and therefore not applying to infidels. Frichner rightly observes that the Doctrine can best be characterized as the Doctrine of Christian Discovery, which she also calls the Doctrine of Domination. The Age of Discovery can be traced to as early as the eleventh century, especially when Pope Urban II in 1095 gave permission for the First Crusade to fight the Muslims in the Holy Land.[5] This is followed by the closing of the land route to the East which consequently obliged Europe to look for alternative routes. This sets off the frenzy for 'discovery' which, in most cases, was also encouraged and justified by papal documents.

II From the papal bulls to international law

Some papal documents called bulls issued in the fifteenth century are to be noted for their importance in using religious reasons to justify plundering resources of other people. The bull *Dum diversas* of 18 June 1452 was written by Pope Nicholas V to King Alfonso of Portugal authorizing an expedition against the Saracens of North Africa. He grants Alfonso the right to confiscate all the lands and property of any Saracen rulers. This bull is seen by some as the one which authorized the Portuguese to carry out slave trading. It says in part: 'we grant to you full and free power, through the Apostolic authority by this edict, to invade, conquer, fight, subjugate the Saracens and pagans and other infidels and other enemies of Christ'.[6] The same pope issued a bull called *Romanus pontifex* on 8 January 1455 to settle the disputes between Portugal and Spain. This bull confirmed Portugal's dominion over all lands discovered by Portugal during the Age of Discovery. It repeats in substance what was written

90

in *Dum diversas* and says '[we grant you power] to invade, search out, capture, vanquish and subdue all Saracens and pagans whatsoever …'[7]

Another pope, Alexander VI (1431–1503) who was from Spain, issued the bull *Inter caetera* on 4 May 1493. The aim of the bull was also to settle the conflict between Spain and Portugal, this time favouring Spain. The pope says: 'by tenor of these presents, should any of said islands have been found by your envoys and captains, [we] give, grant and assign to you and your heirs and successors, kings of Castile and Leon, forever, together with all their dominions'.[8]

With these bulls, we can say that the popes gave all the powers that the rulers of Spain and Portugal needed to colonize and take all the lands that had not yet been, and those that were to be 'discovered' by any other Christian nation, in short, the whole world outside Europe; and to enslave the people found there, and this for perpetuity. Europe was not only 'discovering'; it was also looking for resources, especially after the eastern routes over land had been closed. These bulls and others not cited were to eventually form the basis for what was to be known as the law of nations in which the religious and racial justifications eventually get intertwined.

The cited bulls were later used by colonizing states to justify their actions. Frichner's study is very helpful in this regard in relation to the Americas.[9] She shows how the use of the papal bulls served as a justification of the decisions of the US Supreme Court in 1823 which ruled against natives possessing land in the famous US Supreme Courts ruling *Johnson* v. *M'Intosh 8 Wheat 543* (1823).[10] Marshall based his ruling on many documents including the licence of 5 May 1496 given to Cabot by the King of England.[11] Frichner demonstrates that the US Supreme Court Justice Joseph Story in his *Commentaries* made a direct reference to the already cited papal bull *Inter caetera*.[12] The reasoning is very simple and insidious: the natives lost their right to complete sovereignty because they belonged to countries unknown to Christian people.

III The phenomenon of *poroipiracy* and the destruction of the environment in Africa

With this brief overview on the historical and religious background to the phenomenon of *poroipiracy*, the discussion on the plundering of resources can now focus on more recent events in Africa. The damning report from the UN in 2002 on the looting of the wealth of the Democratic Republic of Congo can be used as an example of *poroipiracy*. The report is a consequence of the UN Security Council request by the Secretary General to establish a Panel of Experts on the Illegal Exploitation of Natural and Other Forms of Wealth in the Democratic Republic of Congo.[13] The report speaks of mass-scale looting, with the illegal exploitation of mineral and forest resources taking place at an alarming rate. This involved the neighbouring countries of Uganda, Rwanda and Burundi.[14]

In 2006, the Edmonds Institute, based in Washington, and the African Centre for Biosafety, based in Richmond, South Africa, released their report *Out of Africa: Mysteries of Access and Benefit Sharing* which documents a widespread illicit taking of and using of genetic materials from Africa.[15] More than 31 of the 54 countries of Africa are cited, including regions like Eastern Africa and Central and West Africa. The materials looted cover diverse areas like multi-purpose medicinal plants, vaccines, cosmetics. Ailments and conditions that can be treated by these resources include diabetes, impotence, infections, drug addiction, obesity and fungal infections.[16]

Beyond the extraction of natural resources from the continent, foreign powers also consider Africa as the dumping ground of their waste. The Trafigura-*Probo Koala* saga is an example of overt environmental racism showing how in this case safeguarding the environment of Africa and health of the Africans do not count. On 19 August 2014, a ship called the *Probo Koala*, registered in Panama, owned by a Greek company and chartered by Trafigura Beheer BV of the Netherlands, offloaded more than 500 tons of toxic waste at the port of Abidjan, Ivory Coast.[17] The gas that was released is blamed for causing 17 deaths and injuring over 30,000 Ivorians. It is said that almost 100,000 Ivorians sought medical help. Trafigura continues to deny any liability in the case.

Another example involving environmental pollution with very serious public health consequences is given by the UN Environment Programme Report of 2011 called *Environmental Assessment of Ogoniland*.[18] It revealed that the area found in Nigeria is even more polluted than was feared. The findings indicate that oil contamination has affected practically all the components of the environment in Ogoniland with the consequence that the ecosystem and public health of the people are heavily compromised. Land-based vegetation is contaminated; the quality of surface and ground water is compromised; the fishing industry is threatened; the soils and sediments are heavily polluted with dire consequences for public health. The negative socio-economic consequences relating to the livelihoods are not difficult to imagine.

From the above, we see how *poroipiracy* that has come to involve African actors sometimes goes with the destruction of the resources and the environment and consequently dehumanizes the victims of exploitation.

IV The response of the African Church

Given the very serious problems that the African continent faces in the way its resources are being looted by outsiders and insiders, the African Church has reacted rather belatedly. At the local level, the Roman Catholic Church in the Democratic Republic of Congo is participating in ensuring that wealth accruing from the resources of the country is equitably used by evaluating the mining contracts. The Centre of Studies for Social Action, a Jesuit organization, has been chosen to coordinate 53 Congolese NGOs involved in good governance of natural resources. The Centre has four thematic groups in four provinces dealing with contracts. Their work consists of raising awareness, organizing workshops and lobbying companies.

In addition to this local initiative, the celebration of the Second Special Assembly for Africa of the Synod of Bishops in 2009 had some points related to the proper use of natural resources. In no. 29 of the 57 final propositions, the bishops note that while thanking God for the abundant riches that God gave to Africa, Africans have become victims of bad management of these resources by local authorities and exploitation by foreign powers. The Synod Fathers condemned the culture of consumerism which is wasteful, advocate a culture of moderation and ask that Church institutions press for allowing populations to enjoy their natural resources.[19]

The Post-Synodal Apostolic Exhortation *Africae munus* followed up this very important issue. In no. 79 of the Exhortation, Pope Benedict XVI asks 'all the members of the Church to work and speak out in favour of an economy that cares for the poor and is resolutely opposed to an unjust order which, under the pretext of reducing poverty, has often helped to aggravate it'.[20] He also notes that God has given Africa important natural resources, but that the continent suffers from chronic poverty, effects of exploitation and embezzlement of funds, both locally and abroad. He recommends that the Church speak out against these injustices in this unjust order.[21]

V Conclusion

The African and universal Church has to courageously address the issue that plundering of the resources of other people is in fact grounded in some of its past official documents. This calls for prophetic courage. It should also critically examine and apologize for having benefited from such *poroipiracy* and, where need arises, offer compensation. Finally, it should lobby multinational companies concerning the proper use and management of African resources.

Notes

1. I have used the term *poroi*, from the Greek, meaning resources, to extend piracy beyond bio-piracy, which refers to resources associated with life, in order to include piracy of inorganic materials like minerals, oil and land.
2. An example of this violence against the native people of the Americas by Europeans can be found in David E. Stannard, *American Holocaust: The Conquest of the New World*, New York, 1992.
3. Tonya Gonella Frichner, 'Preliminary Study of the Impact on Indigenous Peoples of the International Legal Construct Known as the Doctrine of Discovery, which has served as the Foundation of the Violation of their Human Rights', New York, 2010, http://www.un.org/esa/socdev/unpfii/documents/E.C.19.2010.13%20EN.pdf. See also Steven T. Newcomb's book, *Pagans in the Promised Land: Decoding the Doctrine of Christian Discovery*, Golden, CO 2008.
4. Frichner, 'Preliminary Study', p. 4.
5. One will find some documents attributed to Urban II calling upon Christians to join the crusade. Cf. 'Medieval Sourcebook: Urban II (1088–1099): Speech at Council of Clairmont 1095 – Five Versions of the Speech', http://www.fordham.edu/halsall/source/urban2-5vers.html.
6. I have used the translation given at http://unamsanctamcatholicam.blogspot.nl/2011/02/dum-diversas-english-translation.html.
7. For the text in English, see Frances Gardiner Davenport (ed.), *European Treaties Bearing on the History of the United States and Its Dependencies to 1648*, Washington, 1917, pp. 20–6.
8. Davenport (ed.), *European Treaties,* pp. 75–8.
9. Frichner, 'Preliminary Study'.
10. Frichner, 'Preliminary Study, p. 11 and p. 17.
11. The text of the licence can be found at http://www.tudorplace.com.ar/Documents/CabotHenryVIIpatent.htm.
12. Frichner, 'Preliminary Study', p. 24.
13. See 'Report of the Panel of Experts on the Illegal Exploitation of Natural and Other Forms of Wealth in the Democratic Republic of Congo' (S/2001/357), New York, 2001, p. 1.
14. 'Report of the Panel', p. 2.
15. Jay MacGown, *Out of Africa: Mysteries of Access and Benefit Sharing*, Washington, 2006.
16. MacGown, *Out of Africa*, p. iii.

17. A summary of the facts presented here are taken from Greenpeace and Amnesty International, *The Toxic Truth*, Amsterdam, 2012.
18. United Nations Environment Programme, Environmental Assessment of Ogoniland, Nairobi, 2011. Cf. http://postconflict.unep.ch/publications/OEA/UNEP_OEA.pdf.
19. See the text of the propositions at http://www.vatican.va/roman_curia/synod/ documents/rc_synod_doc_20091023_elenco-prop-finali_en.html.
20. Benedict XVI, *Africae munus*, Nairobi, 2011.
21. Benedict XVI, *Africae munus*.

Unemployment in the First World: The US Experience

KENNETH HIMES

Our religious tradition affirms the importance of work and the tragedy of unemployment. In the USA, there has been a growing percentage of the general population that is unemployed and underemployed. The number significantly increased during the Great Recession beginning with the 2007 financial crisis. Today we are far from the goal of full employment that the American Catholic bishops called for in their 1985 Pastoral Letter. Three particular harms of unemployment are noted: the long-term unemployed, the suppression of wage increases and the growth in inequality. The Church must speak and act on behalf of the unemployed.

A discussion of unemployment from the Catholic perspective should be preceded by a reminder of the significance of work in the Bible and in Catholic Social Teaching.

I   Work and the Christian tradition

Both creation accounts found in the Book of Genesis tell us that God placed human beings amid the rest of creation to cultivate and care for it. It is important to note the divine command to work precedes the biblical account of the fall of humankind. After sin enters into Eden the nature of work is that it will involve hard toil and sweat (Gen. 2.17–19), but from the outset human beings were destined to work the land and derive food from it (Gen. 1.28–30; 2.15–16). The commandment to keep the Sabbath further testifies that an ordinary day is to be taken up with labour, but the seventh day is to be set aside (Exod. 31.12–17), just as the Lord God had done in the original act of creation (Gen. 2.2–3).

The Semitic understanding of the dignity of labour stood in stark contrast to classical Greek and Roman attitudes, where leisure was the activity that permitted a person to attain true fulfilment. Wherever labour is disparaged in the Bible or in later Christian writings, it is an indicator of classical Greek influences.

Throughout the Gospels, Jesus, as a faithful Israelite, reflects a thorough familiarity with the world of work. His preaching, particularly the parables, demonstrate knowledge of a variety of occupations, the lives of ordinary workers and the everyday rhythms of work experience. The apostle Paul also illustrates a Jewish sensibility regarding work. He is blunt in his criticism of those in Thessalonika who eschewed work while waiting for an imminent *parousia* (2 Thess. 3.6–12).

The biblical outlook has deeply influenced Catholic Social Teaching. *Rerum novarum* was written precisely to address the plight of workers in the new industrial order; for Leo XIII, 'the condition of the working population is the question of the hour' (n. 44). The focus on the central importance of work remained in the writings of subsequent popes over the decades. John Paul II devoted an entire encyclical, *Laborem exercens*, to the topic where he maintained, 'human work is a key, probably the essential key, to the whole social question' (n. 3).

In 1985, a few years after John Paul II's encyclical on work, the bishops of the USA wrote a major pastoral letter on the US economy, *Economic Justice For All*. A large section of that letter was given over to an analysis of unemployment as a problem to be given priority in any reform of the economy (nos. 136–69).

Simply put, within the Jewish and Christian traditions work is not a curse, even if some aspects of human work are harsh and difficult. The real curse is unemployment. That has been amply demonstrated by the impact upon the unemployed of the Great Recession that began with the financial crisis of 2007. Employment rates in 2014 have not yet returned to the level they were at the beginning of the millennium.[1] The painful reality is that millions of people have been unemployed, and this has led to significant human and economic costs. I will briefly highlight three of those costs.

II Three social problems related to unemployment

1. The long-term unemployed (LTU) are a sub-group that has suffered greatly. These are people without work for 27 weeks or more. In the late spring of 2014 their number was cited as 3.8 million. They are also disproportionately African American, a group that is 10 per cent of the general population but 22 per cent of the long-term unemployed.[2] The number of LTU prior to the recession was about one-third the number in 2014.

LTU workers over 50 have been particularly hard hit. They are too young to retire, with insufficient savings and ineligibility for old age pensions. Yet, the LTU are eyed warily by potential employers who see them requiring salaries that are too high, having outdated skills, lacking flexibility in work hours as well as methods, and posing a risk for high health costs, since in the USA health insurance is primarily provided by employers.

Of course, there is the emotional suffering accompanying being out of work; the 'mounting sense of self-doubt, the awkward silences among friends who grasp for words of comfort'.[3] There is also the financial anxiety of spending savings that wipes out years of work and sacrifice. Perhaps worst of all is the risk of assuming a new identity as 'damaged goods' to prospective employers and 'useless or unnecessary' to oneself. The LTU are people truly marginalized by the present economic situation. They have endured a demeaning blow to human dignity.

2. Surpluses in markets usually drive down costs and the labour market is no exception. Large numbers of unemployed people tend to suppress wages for those with jobs. This is especially the case when, as in the USA, the number of unionized workers with collective bargaining rights has shrunk to less than 7 per cent of the private sector workforce. It is estimated that the Great Recession caused a loss of 8.7 million jobs in the USA. Not until June 2014 did the total number of new jobs climb back to where it was more than six years earlier.

Furthermore, returning to the pre-recession job levels means the US economy is still short of the approximately 6.9 million jobs that were needed to keep pace with population growth since January 2008.[4] So the labour market is still in a condition to suppress wages. And to add to the bad news, many of the lost jobs were in sectors of the economy that traditionally paid higher wages while many of the new jobs are in low-wage sectors.

Ordinarily wages improve when productivity improves. Yet productivity since 2000 has increased nearly 23 per cent in the USA, but the hourly wage of the median worker rose 0.5 per cent. While the recession made things worse for middle-class workers, the trend predates 2007 and is indicative of a longer-term movement in the US economy. Since 1973 productivity is up 80 per cent while the median hourly compensation has increased only 11 per cent. This means that increased profits are going to executives, owners and shareholders, not workers.

Particularly striking is the situation of the working poor. A full-time worker being paid the national minimum wage earned $15,080 in 2014. That is just $650 above the poverty line for a two-person family, leaving very little discretionary income for savings or emergencies. Indeed, many low-wage workers are eligible for government programs such as food stamps that supplement a family food budget. More than 16 million children live in poverty even with a full-time worker in the household.[5]

3. A third negative impact of unemployment is how it exacerbates inequality. Economic inequality has worsened significantly in the USA. The top 1 per cent holds more wealth than the bottom 90 per cent. After the dramatic decline in the financial markets in the recession years there has been a complete recovery but this largely benefits the well-off. The wealthiest 10 per cent got 81 per cent of stock market growth in the recovery. Those wage increases that have occurred in the US economy have happened disproportionately among the already rich. The vast majority of additional household income has gone to the top 1 per cent, and almost all the rest went to the top quintile. The bottom two quintiles have seen no real income growth. The rising tide that supposedly lifts all boats has lifted the yachts but swamped the rowing boats.

Too much concentration of wealth undercuts economic growth according to research sponsored by the International Monetary Fund. The wealthy tend to save and invest rather than purchase consumer goods and services, the areas of the economy where greater demand would create more jobs. When so much income goes to the top, the middle class lacks the purchasing power to keep the economy growing. With restrained economic growth businesses are reluctant to expand and hire new people so unemployment continues.

Taken to an extreme inequality leads to plutocracy, 'the rule by the rich and for the rich'.[6] The present trend towards inequality is not simply the result of market forces despite the claims of neoliberals. There is abundant evidence that policy decisions by federal and state governments have tilted the economic playing field. The de-regulation of banks and other institutions, changes in tax codes, labour laws and corporate governance are just a few of the ways that, in addition to than market forces, have abetted the increased inequality in the USA.

III   What role for the Church?

Historically, American Catholicism has had deep ties with organized labour and working-class people. The Church also established an extensive network of social service agencies and educational institutions that helped the poor achieve upward mobility. Today Catholics span the spectrum of unemployed, blue-collar labourers, middle and upper management, members of the professions and the economic elite. The challenge for the Church has been not to lose touch with the economically vulnerable as the Catholic population diversified.

At the congregational level parishes can assist the unemployed with the marginalization that many jobless people experience by developing programs of peer ministry. Convening local meetings of the unemployed and recently jobless, so they can support and assist one another, is one way to address a pastoral need. Establishing job fairs where local congregants can network, submit applications for work and gather information about job opportunities is also useful. Parishes or dioceses can also host job-hunting workshops that explain search strategies, teach interview skills, assist with writing resumés and offer guidance for salary negotiations.

The openness of the US public square to religious voices has allowed the Church to assume an advocacy role in public policy discussions. The Church can advocate to make work more humane while continuing to be productive and profitable. Whether it is wage subsidies, a rise in the minimum wage linked to inflation for future increases, or an expanded Earned Income Tax Credit, there is a need for proposals that make work worth doing for full-time workers. There is also the need for a 'safety net' that protects those unemployed with medical care, unemployment insurance and assistance in job training and application.

The Church can also remind government leaders of their responsibilities as 'indirect employers', to use the language of John Paul II, to 'conduct a just labour policy'.[7] Perhaps the most important thing the Church in the USA can do is through its preaching and teaching help to 'establish a consensus that everyone has a right to employment. Then the burden of securing full employment falls on all of us – policy makers, business, labour and the general public – to create and implement the mechanism to secure that right.'[8]

To summerize, the Church must join with others to lift the curse of unemployment from the lives of millions of people so each individual may act upon 'the duty to labour faithfully and also the right to work'.[9]

Notes

1. Unemployment statistics in the USA are not precise, since they do not count those who drop out of the labour market and stop looking for work, nor does the official rate reveal the underemployment rate of part-time workers looking for full-time work, nor those not immediately available to return to work, e.g. the sick. Thus, the official rate undercounts the actual number of those desiring a full-time job.
2. Alan Krueger, Aaron Kramer and David Cho, 'Are the Long-Term Unemployed on the Margins of the Labor Market?', http://www.brookings.edu/about/projects/bpea/papers/2014/are-longterm-unemployed-margins-labor-market.
3. Rachel Swarns, 'Nine Months Later, Still Working to Find a Job', *New York Times*, 19 May 2014.
4. Jim Puzzanghera, 'Economy Has Recovered 8.7 Million Jobs Lost in Great Recession', *Los Angeles Times*, 6 June 2014, at http://www.latimes.com/business/la-fi-jobs-20140607-story.html.
5. http://www.childrensdefense.org/policy-priorities/ending-child-poverty/.
6. Francis Fukuyama, 'Left Out', *The American Interest*, 6.3 (2011), available at http://www.the-american-interest.com/article-bd.cfm?piece=906.
7. John Paul II, *Laborem exercens* 17.
8. US Conference of Catholic Bishops, *Economic Justice For All*, n.153, http://www.usccb.org/upload/economic_justice_for_all.pdf.
9. *Gaudium et spes* 67.

Part Three: Theological Forum

The Pope at the Border

DENIS KIM SJ

Pope Francis visited Lampedusa on 8 July 2013. I first saw the event on TV in the evening. It was surprising news. I never expected that the Pope would choose Lampedusa as the site for his first official visit outside of Rome. After all, who cares about Lampedusa, a tiny island off southern Italy, where people, undocumented, from Africa try to enter Europe but where many drown? As a Jesuit and a student of international migration, I was glad to see the Pope urge the world to pay attention to the plight of immigrants as well as show his solidarity with the victims of sea crossing. More than two years passed since his visit. I am now able to see more clearly what his visit means to us, Christians or not.

I   Fortress Europe and marginalized Africa

Lampedusa is a border between Europe and Africa. Dreaming of a better life, Africans attempt to cross by sea to reach Europe without proper documents, leaving Africa behind them. Reportedly, at least 23,000 have died since the year 2000, as they attempted to make it to Europe, and many still continue to die every week. Even knowing the peril of the journey, they still take the risk to migrate. The number of sea crossings has steeply increased, especially as the border control has tightened. Political turmoil after the Arab spring has augmented the numbers. The two disasters after the Pope's visit, in which 400 migrants drowned, led the Italian government to launch its *Mare Nostrum* marine rescue operation in October 2013 rescuing more than 140,000 people, according to the UN High Commissioner for Refugees. Nevertheless, Africans continue this precarious journey to reach Lampedusa. It has become their entry to Europe.

This migration flow is sharply contrasted with another flow: the free movement of European citizens within Europe. Twenty-six European countries, since the Schengen Agreement in 1995, have abolished internal border controls and have established a common visa program, thus allowing these citizens to move freely within this area as in a single country. Their citizens are privileged with the freedom of movement and the opportunity for prosperity. Meanwhile, the EU and its member states have tightened external border control. They have invested in surveillance technology, security forces and detention centres in order to make it harder for 'unwanted' migrants to enter its borders. As a consequence, Europe has become like a fortress: free and secure for insiders, but impenetrable for outsiders. This policy has made Africans take a treacherous journey. The Lampedusa tragedies, as Amnesty International puts aptly, is the 'human cost of Fortress Europe'.

One tends to assume that Africans cross the border in order to pursue a job, security or better opportunities; in other words, to seek their own individual interests. However, migration scholarship advises not to overlook the historical, structural factors that encourage, if not force, migration. First of all, global economic integration has made rapid changes in the 'Global South' and has undermined traditional ways of working and living. People are internally displaced for many reasons. They move to the cities looking for greener pastures yet encounter shortage of jobs. Weak states and poverty lead to lack of human security, violence and human rights violations. All these factors encourage emigration. Second, the post-industrial economy in the 'Global North' has resulted in the de-skilling of labour and the development of new service sectors. Thus, on the one hand, young people who had good educational opportunities do not want to work in 3D (dirty, difficult and dangerous) jobs. On the other, the ageing population has increased and needs care labour. These economic changes have demanded both high- and low-skilled workers. When the demand is not met, it needs workers from outside, i.e. migrants – whether documented or not. Third, at the global level, the development of technologies and transformation as well as cultural practices that transcend borders have promoted mobility. Furthermore, migrants have developed their own informal networks and transnational communities. These networks and communities reinforce migration and facilitated the search for employment and accommodation in the new country. The above factors show that migration is not only a matter of individual decision but an outcome of interconnected and inter-active multi-layered structures.

We live in an age of migration. Human migration is not only the driving force but also a consequence of globalization. Not all migrants, however, are in the same condition. Contemporary migrants have been polarized into two classes: an elite flow and a survival flow. The former includes the flow of professionals and high-skilled transnational workers, whereas the latter is composed of low-skilled workers, such as domestic helpers, nannies, sexual workers etc. People who belong to the former circuits are welcomed almost everywhere and even cause the 'war for talents', whereas those in the latter become 'disposable'. Given this situation, the increase of short-term contract migrant workers is a natural consequence. The Global North wants labour but not labourers. Migrant workers have to return to their home countries after the contracts are over; settlement is not allowed; family accompaniment is prohibited. Indeed, most people who take the risk to arrive in Lampedusa cannot even make this short-term contract and thus cannot but pursue the 'irregular' path. Moreover, we must also register the fact that most refugees never get out of Africa and are hosted in some of the world's poorest countries.

We now see a bigger contrast. In the mainstream media of the West, Africa tends to be described as a synonym for poverty, war, political instability and human rights violations. (My African friends take this kind of representation as another orientalism which functions to justify a Western superiority.) Meanwhile, Europe has proudly enjoyed its affluence, democracy and human rights as it continues to tighten up its borders, preventing any entry of Africans (and others) into its well-guarded territories.

II Indifference and compassion

Lampedusa is not merely a border between Africa and Europe. The Pope made a pastoral visit after a tragedy. He went 'to pray and to offer a sign of my closeness [to the victims], but also to challenge our consciences lest this tragedy be repeated'. In his poignant homily, he challenged the globalization of indifference and called for the recovery of the ability to weep in front of others' suffering. Inadvertently, thus, he has made Lampedusa a border between indifference and compassion.

The Pope mentioned Herod who killed the children in Bethlehem, but with a nuanced comment that 'Herod sowed death to protect his own

106

comfort, his own soap bubble'. He gently suggests that Herod's insecurity about his own comfort led him to be cruel, to make others suffer, and that we all have a Herod that 'lurks in our heart'. Thus, by comparing Herod and Rachel who wept for her lost children, he alluded to the comfortable life in Europe in front of others' sorrow. The Pope's comment is touching. We can hear a similar voice in the 2014 report of Amnesty International, when it argues that EU policy puts refugees and migrants at risk by preventing them from seeking asylum. Amnesty International implies that EU policy, oriented towards a Fortress Europe, drives Africans to death, just as Herod did. It challenges the EU to open its doors to more humanistic policies just as the Pope exhorts that people need to open their hearts to migrants who face closed borders.

The theme of the globalization of indifference is repeated in *Evangelii gaudium*, the Pope's first apostolic exhortation, published a few months after his visit to Lampedusa. In this exhortation, the Pope mentions 'indifference' four times. Interestingly, he does so twice in the context of economy and twice in relation to general culture. He is especially critical of the contemporary economy, based on the free market, economic growth or trickle-down theory, arguing that it has resulted in exclusion, inequality and indifference. While people enjoy prosperity and consumerist culture, a globalization of indifference grows cancerously. Then, people 'end up being incapable of feeling compassion at the outcry of the poor, weeping for other people's pain, … as though all this were someone else's responsibility and not our own' (*EG* 54). Thus, indifference is not just an individual moral quality, but also a cultural condition on which exclusion is built.

Lampedusa is a site to face the consequences of indifference in the contemporary world. Ironically, it is the reason why the world was so impressed by the visit of the Pope. Like me, many people, even those who have little interest in the Church, were surprised. Local people in Lampedusa were among them. A media article delivered a local response: 'It was not even thinkable that the pope would come to an Island like this one.' It described 'a banner draped along the pope's route read: "Welcome among the *ultimi*" – a word in Italian that has connotations of both furthest and least'. Thus, Lampedusa exists not only in southern Italy. It also exists wherever there are *ultimi*.

Perhaps more than the local population in Lampedusa, I was thrilled by watching the Pope, through the screen, during his visit to Korea in

2014. On 16 August, during his car parade amid a million people cheering before the beatification mass of the Korean martyrs, the Pope stopped his car at one point. It was unscheduled, but he did it in order to meet the victims' families of the sunken ferry *Sewol* in April. It was (and still is) a politically sensitive action, because these families struggled to demand a due investigation of the sinking and to find justice. Being aware of the layers of meaning behind the Pope's gestures, I was exhilarated when he stopped and met them. At that moment, an image leaped into my mind, that of the Pope's stopping and praying on his way to Bethlehem during his visit to the Middle East (24–26 May 2014) at the concrete barrier which Israel has built in and around the West Bank. Later, during an interview on his return flight, he was asked about the political meaning of his encounter with the families, and he replied: 'There is no neutral position in front of human suffering!'

III   The Church as a field hospital

I do not know how the Pope came to choose Lampedusa as the site for his first visit outside of Rome. First things – first words, first gestures, first visits – are important ways of showing priorities. Then, what better place than Lampedusa would indicate the Pope's vision of the Church as a 'field hospital after battle'? The migrants who make it there are the wounded after a battle of life and death.

In his interview with *La Civiltà Cattolica* on his vision of the Church, the Pope made it clear that 'organizational and structural reforms are secondary' and '[the] first reform must be the attitude'. Indeed, the reform most needed is one of attitudes, a reform that calls for the commitment of all Christians. Needless to say, it has to begin with church leadership. It is heart-warming to know a bishop in a poor mission area of Asia who replaced his car with a smaller one. Certainly, it is part of what is now called the 'Pope Francis effect'! But more is needed, and church leaders, starting with bishops and priests, need to go to the many Lampedusas in today's world. Being present at the borders, where people strive for human dignity and rights, peace and reconciliation in the midst of systemic violence, discrimination and hatred, church leaders would then better understand the signs that read: 'Welcome among the *ultimi*'! Among the *ultimi* is indeed where Pope Francis is leading the Church to be in today's world.

Ukrainian Maidan:
The Civil Mobilization for Dignity and the Religious Situation in Ukraine

JOSÉ CASANOVA

On 22 January 2014, an official delegation of the Council of the Religious Communities of Ukraine visited Ukraine's President Viktor Yanukovych with two main petitions. The first was an urgent demand that the government and security forces should use maximum restraint in order to avoid bloodshed and violence in responding to the Maidan protest movement and that a maximum effort should be made to ensure that the conflict and the confrontation between the government and the Maidan movement be resolved through peaceful negotiations and political dialogue. The second petition was actually an offer of mediation, whereby all the religious communities of Ukraine expressed their readiness to serve as bona fide mediators between the government and the opposition and between all the social and political forces.

Striking about the delegation was the fact that it was composed of high representatives of all the religious communities of Ukraine. There were representatives of the three Orthodox churches as well as of the Ukrainian Catholic Church, that is, of the four national Eastern Rite churches. There were also official representatives of all the other Christian communities of Ukraine: of the Roman Catholic Church as well as of the three main communities from the Reformed tradition – the Evangelical Lutheran Church, the Association of Ukrainian Baptists and the Ukrainian Association of Pentecostal Assemblies. In addition, there were also representatives of the Jewish and Muslim communities of Ukraine. Each and all of the representatives of such an unusual pluralist and ecumenical body spoke in unison in support of the main demand for the peaceful and negotiated resolution to the conflict. This at a time when the government had announced plans to pass legislation at the Ukrainian National Assembly that would basically decriminalize the increasingly violent crackdowns of the security forces while criminalizing any Maidan-like peaceful civil activities.

Fortuitously, the Ukrainian Orthodox Church-Moscow Patriarchate (UOC-MP), the largest religious community of Ukraine and the one closest to the Yanukovych regime, occupied at the time the rotating presidency of the council of religious communities and therefore felt compelled somewhat reluctantly to lead the delegation and support its demands. The religious situation in Ukraine had been radically different only 25 years earlier, before Gorbachev's glasnost policies arrived finally also in Ukraine in 1989. At the time, the Russian Orthodox Church was the only officially recognized Church in Ukraine, claiming canonical hegemony over the entire Soviet territory.

In the fall of 1989, two other historical Ukrainian churches, the Ukrainian Greek Catholic Church (UGCC) and the Ukrainian Autocaephalous Orthodox Church (UAOC), that had been proscribed and persecuted by Stalin and the Soviet regime since 1945, began to re-emerge publicly from the underground in Western Ukraine. Throughout the region, confronted with the slow response of the communist authorities to their demands, the faithful began to take affairs in their own hands by switching the allegiance of their parishes to the re-established churches. In order to counter the nationalist appeal of its two historical competitors, in January 1990 the Russian Orthodox Church was officially renamed the Ukrainian Orthodox Church. As the politics of Ukrainian independence spilled over into the ecclesiastical sphere, there emerged a movement for independence of Ukrainian Orthodoxy from Moscow, which was supported by religious as well as secular Ukrainian elites. This revived the age-old rivalry between Orthodox Kyiv and Orthodox Moscow, leading to the establishment of the competing Ukrainian Orthodox Church-Kyiv Patriarchate (UOC-KP), which so far has not gained canonical recognition by any other Orthodox Church and the Ukrainian Orthodox Church-Moscow Patriarchate (UOC-MP).

Consequently, by 1992, there were four competing national churches in Ukraine, three Orthodox and one Uniate or Eastern Catholic, all claiming to be the legitimate heir of the Kyivan Rus Church, all claiming the title of the Metropolitan of Kyiv and all Rus and thus laying claim also to be the legitimate Church of the Ukrainian nation and of the entire Ukrainian territory. Although there is some competitive presence of all four churches in all regions of Ukraine, they are diversely distributed across the Ukrainian territory, and therefore none of them can claim real hegemony over the entire Ukrainian nation.

Least competitive and pluralistic are the eastern and southern oblasts, where the Moscow Patriarchate has dominance. But there the overwhelming majority of the population still remains 'unaffiliated' or unchurched. Paradoxically, Western Ukraine, which had been historically, at least since the eighteenth century, the territorial monopoly of the Ukrainian Catholic Church, remains the most religious region of Ukraine, but also the religiously most dynamic, most competitive and most pluralistic. By early 1991, the UGCC had regained its historical predominant position in the three Galician oblasts of Lviv, Ivano-Frankivsk and Ternopil. Yet, its traditional territorial monopoly in Halychena has been broken, as a significant number of priests and parishes chose to remain Orthodox, while often transferring their allegiance from the Moscow Patriarchate to either the UOC-KP or the UAOC.

Besides the competition of the four 'national' churches, one finds in Western Ukraine the active presence of all other religious organizations, Roman Catholic as well as the various Protestant groups, Jewish as well as Muslim and other new religious movements. Although it comprises just 15 per cent of the population of Ukraine, the seven Western oblasts together contain almost 40 per cent of all its religious communities. The five Eastern oblasts by contrast comprise 27 per cent of the population of Ukraine but contain less than 15 per cent of its religious communities.

Besides the various branches of Eastern Christianity and Catholicism, Ukraine has also had an active Baptist presence since the nineteenth century. It became in fact the Bible Belt of the Soviet Union, serving as home to half of all registered Baptists in the USSR, 1.5 million strong, while the underground Baptist community was estimated at three million by the 1950s. It was in fact the largest Baptist community in all of Europe. After the fall of the Soviet Union, Ukraine became the centre of evangelical publishing, seminary training and missionary recruiting for much of Eurasia. There has been an equally remarkable growth of Pentecostal congregations. While constituting only two per cent of the population, by 2000 one-fourth of all registered places of worship in

Ukraine were Protestant. In Southeastern Ukraine the number of Protestant churches nearly equalled the number of Orthodox churches. Ukraine also has the largest mega-church of Europe, an independent Pentecostal church founded in Kyiv in 1994 with over 25,000 members. In the same way as the Ukrainian Catholic Church has served as a destabilizing factor in the formation of Ukrainian Orthodox confessionalism, the dramatic growth of Ukrainian Protestant churches has played a destabilizing factor in the identification of modern Ukraine with the Christianity of Kyivan Rus. Moreover, while Ukrainian Catholics and Protestants together may constitute no more than 10 per cent of the Ukrainian population, on any given Sunday there may be as many of them in church as there are Orthodox faithful, although the Orthodox population may be six times larger.

The post-Soviet revival and growth of Jewish religious communities and of Muslim communities, particularly of Crimean Tatars, has also contributed to greater pluralization beyond Christianity. Moreover, with the institutionalization of a Ukrainian secular constitutional state, based on the dual principle of 'no establishment' and 'free exercise of religion', the very distinctions between 'church' and 'sect', between 'national confession' and 'religious minorities', or between 'traditional' and 'foreign' religions tend to disappear, and all the religious communities in Ukraine, churches as well as sects, Christian and non-Christian, have become denominations. Ukraine is today the only country in Europe with a denominational pattern of religious pluralism akin to the United States.

Most striking is the fact that in the last two decades all the religious communities of Ukraine have been consistently growing year by year in terms of membership affiliation, number of religious communities, ministers and vocations, Sunday schools and most other institutional indicators. The only figures that have decreased consistently year by year have been the numbers of 'unaffiliated', 'non-believers' and 'atheists'. In this respect, Ukraine has undergone since independence an extraordinary religious revival, more pronounced than that of any other post-Soviet society.

Equally striking is the relative absence of serious interreligious strife despite the competitive pluralization. With the exception perhaps of the Moscow Patriarchate, which still claims canonical jurisdiction over the entire territory of Ukraine and often rants against 'Uniatists', non-canonical Orthodox 'schismatics' and Protestant 'heretics', the relative ecumenical interreligious recognition of all the religious communities of Ukraine is made evident by the very existence of the Council of Religious Communities with a rotating presidency and their disposition to form a joint delegation in order to present the above mentioned demands to the government.

This interreligious recognition and respect was actually enhanced by the experience of Maidan, when for several months priests, pastors, rabbis and representatives of practically all the religious communities of Ukraine found themselves side by side ministering to the spiritual and material needs of the hundreds of thousands of Ukrainian citizens, members from all the religious communities, who under harsh conditions had maintained a continuous mobilization against the policies of the regime. Almost as if echoing the instructions of Pope Francis, religious pastors had left the comfort of their own temples and had gone to the public square to accompany the people and to serve their needs, in the process literally absorbing the smell of sheep, of the people who for months had lived in tents in sub-zero temperatures. Once the violent crackdown began a few weeks after their failed delegation, the churches became literally field hospitals in the midst of battle, attending to the wounded and, once the massacre of mostly unarmed civilians began, giving the last rites to the dead and leading ecumenical funeral services.

After the fall of the Yanukovych regime all conflict and violence came to an end in Kyiv despite the Russian propaganda concerning the revolutionary takeover by violent 'fascists and anti-semites'. But the violence – indeed, open military aggression – began in earnest now in Crimea and in the Eastern oblasts of Ukraine, particularly in Luhansk and Donetsk. Crimea was annexed by Russia through military force, while the most eastern regions of Luhansk and Donetsk bordering on Russia have been for several months, and still remain today, a war zone. In Crimea, the Russian Orthodox Church re-established its territorial hegemony, while other religious communities, particularly the Muslim Crimean Tatars, who can claim most rightly to be the legitimate 'native' inhabitants of Crimea, and Roman Catholics, Ukrainian Catholics, Orthodox 'schismatics' and Protestant 'heretics' have been harassed and proscribed. Many of their ministers and religious leaders had to go into exile. Those who remained had either to apply for a Russian passport or be registered as 'foreign agents'. A similar situation emerged in the occupied territories of Luhansk and Donetsk.

In Ukraine itself, the two main Orthodox churches, claiming allegiance respectively to the Moscow and the Kyiv Patriarchate, are unlikely to either reunite freely or to absorb each other through hostile competition. Much less should one anticipate the amicable or hostile absorption of the Ukrainian Catholic Church by Orthodoxy. Given the diverging orientation of the Ukrainian Churches of the Kyivan tradition respectively to Moscow, Constantinople and Rome, barring the ecumenical reconciliation between the three Romes, one can expect that Ukraine will remain a vital ecumenical battleground for all three, fuelling the competition between them. While full ecumenical reconciliation between the three Romes may be far off, within Ukraine itself a more plausible and ecumenically positive development may actually take place. As in the USA, denominational competition is likely to lead to de facto recognition of each other as sister churches. Something of this ecumenical praxis was already visible at Maidan.

Reconciliation of the same sister churches across the lands of Kyievan Rus – Ukraine, Belarus and Russia – is going to be a much more difficult task. But the Ukrainian Catholic Church, at least, is committed to such a path. It is now preparing the millennial celebration of the martyrdom of Saints Borys and Hlib in 2015 as an opportunity to preach the Christian duty of peace-making. Borys and Hlib were murdered by their brother Sviatopolsk in the succession struggles after the death of their father Volodomyr the Great. Soon their exemplary death, refusing to draw the sword against their own brother, became the cause of a popular veneration that stressed Christian peace-making in violent times. President Putin has decided not to sponsor such a millennial celebration within the Russian Federation, claiming that the martyrdom of Borys and Hlib for the sake of peace cannot serve as exemplary at a time when people are being mobilized to go to war for their countries.

An Extraordinary Synod on the Family – But Where Were the Women?

TINA BEATTIE

The Extraordinary Synod on the Family took place over two weeks in Rome in October 2014. It was the first of two such Synods initiated by Pope Francis. The Synod in October 2015 will be the culmination of the process that has now begun, where decisions will be made about changes in the Church's pastoral practice (which seems certain) and possible changes in the Church's teaching. This seems less certain, though as Cardinal Reinhard Marx pointed out during the Synod, church doctrine can and does change.[1]

The build-up to the Synod was a time of mixed messages, beginning with the questionnaire that was distributed by the Vatican to bishops' conferences around the world as part of a preparatory document,[2] with encouragement to solicit as many responses as possible on questions ranging from natural law, contraception and marriage to homosexuality, divorce and changing sexual attitudes in different cultures. The questionnaire was poorly worded, but thousands of Catholics around the world answered it, delighted with the novelty of being consulted about such issues.

The bishops' conferences were asked by the Vatican not to publish the results, but the German and Swiss conferences published candid summaries of the range of responses.[3] These indicated that, while respect for marriage was high, there was a desire for a more compassionate way of dealing with divorced and remarried Catholics through readmission to the sacraments. There was relatively little support for same-sex marriage, but significant support for civil partnerships and for the idea that same-sex relationships should find a space of affirmation and blessing within the Church. The Church's teachings on contraception, homosexuality, cohabitation and natural law were almost universally ignored or rejected.

The Vatican published an *Instrumentum laboris* based on responses to the questionnaire.[4] This discusses a comprehensive range of challenges to marriage and family life that arise from a plurality of different cultural and social contexts and situations of violence and poverty. However, while acknowledging widespread resistance to some aspects of the Church's teachings on sexuality, it tends to attribute this to poor formation and secular influences rather than questioning the legitimacy and relevance of the teachings themselves. Though only referring to it once explicitly, the document's representation of marriage and the family resonates with the language of 'theology of the body', a movement based on Pope John Paul II's catechesis on the Book of Genesis and widely promoted throughout the Church.

This constitutes the background to the Synod, which was attended by nearly 200 bishops and cardinals, 25 couples and several observers from other churches. From the outset, Pope Francis urged the assembled prelates to speak freely, using the Greek word *parrhesia* to describe the candour and courage that he hoped for.

They took him at his word. Rarely has there been such a sense of the global diversity of the Catholic Church on display before the eyes of the world. As one commentator observed, 'Ironically, by choosing what may have seemed a gentle topic, Pope Francis unleashed a torrent of words over some of the most complex issues in the Church. No one can say that the Synod did not take up matters that were of great concern to Catholics.'[5]

The Western media tended to focus on issues of marriage and divorce and same-sex relationships, but the discussions were much wider than that. From Asia came stories of economic deprivation and migration and also of mixed marriages and arranged marriages. From Africa came questions of polygamy and poverty as well as numerous other cultural practices. A common theme was the threat that individualism and isolationism poses to the family, but for some delegates from the global South, the problem was more a lack of solitude and privacy that comes from overcrowding. The language in which church teaching is framed was a central concern. The majority advocated pastorally sensitive language when dealing with the complex realities of human love and sexuality, but a minority insisted that the Church must state her teaching unequivocally and authoritatively. As far as I could see, there were few if any references to theology of the body, except for some of the married couples who were clearly chosen because of their support for this and for natural family planning. On the other hand, neither does there seem to have been a robust questioning of the teachings of *Humanae vitae*, which responses to the questionnaires surely invited.

An interim document – the *Relatio post disceptationem*[6] – was published after the first week. This created consternation among some members of the hierarchy for what they saw as its excessively conciliatory approach to pastoral dilemmas.[7] It sought a conciliatory way forward for divorced and remarried Catholics, it spoke of 'welcoming homosexual persons', and it acknowledged the positive aspects of civil unions, cohabitation and same-sex couples, while being careful not to compromise church teaching. In the ensuing furore, the English translation was changed from 'Welcoming homosexual persons' to 'Providing for homosexual persons'. The Italian – which remained unchanged – was '*Accogliere le persone omossesuali*'.

The final report is to serve as a working document in preparation for next year's more decisive Synod.[8] For those hoping for a continuation of the radical wording of the interim document, this second one was a disappointment. Three paragraphs dealing with gay relationships and divorce and remarriage failed to gain the required two-thirds majority from the 183 prelates who voted, though they all still had a majority in favour. However, in the remarkable spirit of openness that characterized the Synod, Pope Francis insisted that the excluded paragraphs should be included in the final document, with voting figures published for all the paragraphs. There is a delicious irony at work in this, because if one publishes the excluded paragraphs in a working document, in what meaningful sense can one say they have been excluded? Everything is up for discussion. Nothing has, in fact, been excluded.

With that in mind, I would identify two major challenges which I hope will be high on the agenda of those planning for next year's Synod. The first is the absence of women, and the second is the West and the rest.

How was it possible for more than 200 people to spend two weeks discussing the family, with no women representatives apart from those who spoke as half of a couple carefully selected for its conformity to the Church's vision of 'the family'? This is not to deny that some raised issues concerning those who might be in 'irregular relationships' or who might have gay children, but even so, these couples were speaking as and for the normative and narrow model of what it means to be a Catholic family. As a woman journalist observed to me, 'Women are speaking only as couples. But couples don't speak. Only men and women can speak.' It is imperative that all of us, men as well as women, speak out forcefully and persistently about the need for a much greater female presence at the 2015 Synod. This must be not just a censored selection of dutiful handmaidens, but a robust and informed range of participants capable of speaking on behalf of the vast diversity of women and girls who make up the global Church. These participants must be given the same encouragement that Pope Francis gave to the bishops and cardinals – to speak with *parrhesia* about the challenges and struggles faced by Catholic women today and the insights we bring to the Church. Francis has repeatedly acknowledged the need to include women more fully in church institutions and structures. His credibility has been undermined by his failure to include women at the 2014 Synod, and it is imperative that he does not repeat the same mistake in 2015.

Another vital and related challenge is that of bridging the gulf between the West and the rest. This will require recognizing that the Church truly is a living body that flourishes through unity in diversity. But what is the cost of unity, and how much diversity can be accommodated? That is a challenge to all sides. This was a Synod that brought together bishops from across the world's cultures and contexts. It served as a reminder that the unity of the Catholic Church is a liturgical and sacramental unity, not a moral and cultural unity.

By the end of the Synod, it was clear that the African bishops in particular had staked their claim to a say in the Church's teachings, often in opposition to their more liberal European counterparts.[9] Nigerian Archbishop Ignatius Jos Kaigama spoke eloquently about Africa's coming of age.[10] He said that Africa does not need international organizations imposing their Western ideas and policies, including their liberal sexual ethics, on African cultures and traditions. Many African women theologians and activists point out that such appeals to culture and tradition often mask attitudes of male domination that are detrimental to women and girls. However, the Archbishop was surely right when he insisted that what Africa needs is access to education and economic justice. If we in the West ignore these needs by speaking as if sexual rights come before every other right, we should not be surprised if a rift opens up between Catholicism of the Global South and that of the Western democracies.

Reflecting on these issues, I find myself returning again and again to Pope Francis' insistence on the Church of the Poor. If we can find consensus on tackling social and economic injustice, then we can ask in what ways females and gay people are particularly affected by injustices that stem from poverty, lack of education, sexual abuse and stigmatization. But if we focus instead on carte blanche issues of women's rights or gay rights, we risk promoting an agenda heavily biased towards a liberal Western elite which, in 50 years of gradually accumulated individual rights, including sexual rights, has done nothing to turn the tide of social and economic injustice. The era of individual rights in the West has been accompanied by the rise of a political system that is utterly servile to corporate interests and bereft of any vision of justice or the common good.

So there is much work to be done, but this Synod has started a remarkable process. Until the election of Pope Francis, it would have been almost impossible to imagine an event like this. The sclerosis of authoritarianism, the censoriousness of the CDF, the sense of scandal, corruption, cowardice and defensiveness infecting the hierarchy, these were all signs of a Church suffering from a profound sickness of the soul that would surely take generations to heal, if it were not – as some would argue – a Church in terminal decline. When Francis was elected, many of us were as incredulous as we were elated and that incredulity quickly gave way to scepticism. He is a master rhetorician, a consummate story teller who intuitively understands the power of symbols and gestures to transform beautiful words into deeply moving and meaningful acts of solidarity, compassion and humour. But is there any more to him than that? Is it all style and no substance? The Synod has answered that question. Pope Francis is a true radical – going to the roots of the Catholic faith, encouraging a spirit of freedom in faith that is willing to take risks, to make mistakes, to boldly go where others have not dared. He is also a leader who leads from behind, who listens and reflects before he acts. Let's make sure that, by October 2015, he has learned to listen to women as carefully and attentively as he listened to the men at the Synod.

Notes

1. Joshua J. McElwee, 'Cardinal Marx: Doctrine can develop, change', *National Catholic Reporter*, 17 October 2014, http://ncronline.org/news/vatican/cardinal-marx-doctrine-can-develop-change. There was extensive coverage of the Synod on a number of websites and blogs as well as in the printed media. I refer mainly here to Joshua McElwee's daily reports, because they provided the most extensive and consistent coverage.
2. Synod of Bishops, 'III Extraordinary General Assembly: Pastoral Challenges to the Family in the Context of Evangelization – Preparatory Document', 2013, http://www.vatican.va/roman_curia/synod/documents/rc_synod_doc_20131105_iii-assemblea-sinodo-vescovi_en.html.

3. The German bishops' report can be downloaded from the NCR website: http://ncronline.
org/news/global/synod-family-surveys-german-swiss-catholics-reject-teachings-
marriage-sexuality. See also John Wilkins, 'Great Expectations: Pope Francis & the Synod
on the Family', *Commonweal*, 10 September 2014, https://www.commonwealmagazine.
org/great-expectations.
4. Synod of Bishops, 'III Extraordinary General Assembly: Pastoral Challenges to the
Family in the Context of Evangelization – *Instrumentum laboris*', 2014, http://www.
vatican.va/roman_curia/synod/documents/rc_synod_doc_20140626_instrumentum-
laboris-familia_en.html.
5. James Martin, 'What the Synod of Bishops that discussed divorced, LGBT Catholics
did – and didn't – do', *The Daily Mail Online*, 23 October 2014, at http://www.dailymail.
co.uk/wires/reuters/article-2805178/What-Synod-Bishops-discussed-divorced-LGBT-
Catholics-did--didnt--do.html.
6. Holy See Press Office, 'Synod 14 – Eleventh General Assembly: "Relatio post
disceptationem" of the General Rapporteur, Card. Péter Erdö', 13 October 2014, at http://
press.vatican.va/content/salastampa/en/bollettino/pubblico/2014/10/13/0751/03037.html.
7. See Joshua J. McElwee, 'Bishops Critique Synod Document, Saying It May Cause
Confusion', *National Catholic Reporter*, 14 October 2014, http://ncronline.org/blogs/ncr-
today/bishops-critique-synod-document-saying-it-may-cause-confusion.
8. Holy See Press Office, 'Synod 14 – Relatio Synodi of the III Extraordinary General
Assembly of the Synod of Bishops: Pastoral Challenges to the Family in the Context of
Evangelization' (5–19 October 2014), 18 October 2014, http://press.vatican.va/content/
salastampa/en/bollettino/pubblico/2014/10/18/0770/03044.html.
9. Cf. John L. Allen Jr., 'Africans are no longer junior partners in Catholicism Inc.', *Crux*,
17 October 2014, http://www.cruxnow.com/church/2014/10/17/africans-are-no-longer-
junior-partners-in-catholicism-inc/.
10. Cf. Inés San Martin, 'Africans to Westerners at synod: We've got our own problems',
Crux, 1 October 2014, http://www.cruxnow.com/church/2014/10/10/africans-to-
westerners-at-synod-weve-got-our-own-problems/.

Contributors

PAULO FERNANDO CARNEIRO DE ANDRADE is a lay theologian, possessing a Doctorate in Theology from the Pontifical Gregorian University in Rome. He has been teaching in the Ecclesiastical Faculty of Theology of the Pontifical Catholic University in Rio de Janeiro since 1989 and is currently Dean of the Centre for Theology and Social Sciences. Previously he was the President of SOTER – the Brazilian Society of Theology and Science of Religion – and Vice President of INSeCT – the International Network of Societies for Catholic Theology.

Address: Pontifícia Universidade Católica do Rio de Janeiro
Faculdade Eclesiática de Teologia
Rua Marquês de São Vicente, 225
Edificio Cardeal Leme 11 andar
Caixa Postal: 38097 22453-900
Rio de Janeiro, Brazil
Email: paulof@puc-rio.br

TINA BEATTIE is Professor of Catholic Studies and Director of the Digby Stuart Research Centre for Religion, Society and Human Flourishing at the University of Roehampton in London. Her teaching and research interests include gender and sacramentality, women's rights, Catholic social teaching, theology and psychoanalysis and Marian theology and art. Her most recent book is *Theology after Postmodernity – Divining the Void: A Lacanian Reading of Thomas Aquinas* (Oxford, 2013). She is currently undertaking research on maternal wellbeing, poverty and religion.

Address: School of Arts – Digby Stuart College
Roehampton University
Roehampton Lane
London, SW 155PH, United Kingdom
Email: T.Beattie@roehampton.ac.uk

Contributors

JOSÉ CASANOVA is Professor of Sociology and Senior Fellow at the Berkley Center for Religion, Peace and World Affairs at Georgetown University, where he heads the Program on Religion, Globalization and the Secular. His best-known work, *Public Religions in the Modern World* (Chicago, 1994), has become a modern classic in the field and has been translated into six languages, including Japanese, Arabic and Turkish and is forthcoming in Indonesian, Farsi and Chinese. He is also the author of *Europa's Angst vor der Religion* (Berlin, 2009) and *Genealogías de la Secularización* (Barcelona, 2012).

Address: Berkley Center for Religion, Peace and World Affairs
3307 M St NW, Suite 200
Washington, DC, 20007, USA
Email: jvc26@georgetown.edu

GEMMA TULUD CRUZ is Senior Lecturer in Theology at the Australian Catholic University. She is author of *An Intercultural Theology of Migration: Pilgrims in the Wilderness* (2010) and *Toward a Theology of Migration: Social Justice and Religious Experience* (2014). Work on this article was supported by the Australian Catholic University Research Fund (ACURF).

Address: School of Theology
Australian Catholic University
Locked Bag 4115
Fitzroy MDC VIC, 3065, Australia
Email: gemma.cruz@acu.edu.au

ETIENNE GRIEU SJ teaches at the Centre Sèvres (Jesuit Faculties of Paris). His publications include: *Born of God: A Path for Committed Christians, An Essay in Theological Reading* (Paris: Cerf, coll. 'Cogitatio Fidei', 2003); *Such a Strong Bond: When the Love of God is like that of a Deacon* (Paris, L'Atelier, 2012). He was heavily involved in the preparation of the 'Diaconia 2013', an event for the dioceses of France.

Address: Centre Sèvres
35 bis rue de Sèvres
75006 Paris, France
Email: etienne.grieu@centresevres.c

KENNETH HIMES, OFM is Associate Professor in the Theology Department of Boston College.

Address: Theology Department – Boston College
140 Commonwealth Avenue
Chestnut Hill, MA, 02467, USA
Email: Kenneth.himes@bc.edu

PETER KANYANDAGO is a priest from the Archdiocese of Mbarara in Uganda. He is the Director of Research and Professor of Ethics and Developments in the Institute of Ethics and Development Studies at Ugandan Martyrs University.

Address: Institute of Ethics and Development Studies
Ugandan Martyrs University
PO Box 5498
Kampala, Uganda
E-mail: pkanyandago@gmail.com

DENIS KIM SJ has a member of the Society of Jesus since 1991 and was ordained a priest in 2000. He is a Professor of the Faculty of Social Science at the Gregorian University in Rome. Previously, he served as a Professor of the Department of Sociology at Sogang University in Seoul, South Korea (2008–13); Coordinator for the Social Apostolate of the Jesuit Conference of Asia Pacific (2007–13); and Director of Jesuit Refugee Service in East Timor (2001–2).

Address: Pontifical Gregorian University
Piazza della Pilotta 4
00187 Roma, Italy
Email: smilesj@unigre.it

MARYANN CUSIMANO LOVE is an Associate Professor of International Relations in the Politics Department of The Catholic University of America in Washington, DC. She served as a Fellow at the Commission on International Religious Freedom, where she is working with the Foreign Service Institute in creating new training and education materials on religion and foreign policy. Her recent International Relations books include *Beyond Sovereignty: Issues for a Global Agenda* (4th edition, 2011) and *Morality Matters: Ethics and the War on Terrorism* (forthcoming). She serves at the US Catholic Bishops' International Justice and Peace Committee; the Advisory Board of the Catholic Peacebuilding Network; and the Board and Communications Committee of Jesuit Refugee Services. She lives on the Chesapeake Bay outside of Washington DC with her husband Richard and three young children, Maria, Ricky and Ava, who inspired her *New York Times* best-selling children's books, *You Are My I Love You*, *You Are My Miracle*, *You Are My Wish*, *You Are My Wonders* and *Sleep, Baby, Sleep*.

Address: Department of Politics
The Catholic University of America
620 Michigan Ave, NE
Washington, DC 20064, USA
Email: mcusimanolove@comcast.net

FRANCISCO OROFINO AND CARLOS MESTERS are part of CEBI and work as tutors with popular study groups and base ecclesial communities.

Address: Centro de Estudos Bíblicos (CEBI)
CNPJ: 29.832.607/0001-10
CEP: 93121-970
Caixa Postal: 1051
São Leopoldo – RS – Brasil
Email: cmesters@ocarm.org

RONILSO PACHECO is studying theology at the Pontifical Catholic University in Rio de Janeiro (PUC–Rio) and works as a social intermediary for churches and social movements at the NGO Viva Rio. He is a researcher on the CNPq/PUC-Rio academic initiation programme, studying ethics, otherness and spirituality in Emmanuel Lévinas. He is a member of the FALE ('Speak') network, a Christian network for the defence of rights, with a focus on actions to combat violence, racism and the criminalization of poverty.

Address: Rua Conselheiro Ferraz, 30, Ap 203
Lins de Vasconcelos, Rio de Janeiro – RJ

CEP 20710–350, Brazil
Email: ronilsoe_linguagem@yahoo.com.br

JUNG MO SUNG is a Catholic layman. Korean by birth and naturalized Brazilian, he is a professor on the post-graduate course in religious studies at the Methodist University of São Paulo, Brazil. He does research into the relationship between theology, economics and education. He is the author of 18 books, including *Desire, Market and Religion*; *Subject, Capitalism and Religion*; *Beyond the Spirit of Empire* (with J. Rieger and N. Míguez).

Address: Universidade Metodista de São Paulo
Rua Alfeu Tavares, 149 – Rudge Ramos
São Bernardo do Campo – SP, 09641-000, Brazil
Email: jungmosung@gmail.com

GERALD O. WEST is a Senior Professor of Religion, Philosophy and Classics. He has published more than 140 academic essays and articles and authored or edited ten books. He is currently the editor of *Semeia Studies* (a book series of the Society of Biblical Literature, Atlanta, USA) and the *Journal of Theology for Southern Africa* (academic journal based in South Africa). He was awarded the University's Vice-Chancellor's Award, the DVC's Award for Research Excellence in 2012 and was made fellow of the University of KwaZulu-Natal in 2013. He has been involved in the work of Ujamaa Centre for Community Development and Research since it was established in 1989 and served as its Director from 1994 to 2011.

Address: School of Religion, Philosophy and Classics
University of KwaZulu-Natal
King George V Ave, Glenwood
Durban, 4041, South Africa
Email: west@ukzn.ac.za

CONCILIUM
International Journal of Theology

FOUNDERS
Anton van den Boogaard; Paul Brand; Yves Congar, OP; Hans Küng;
Johann Baptist Metz; Karl Rahner, SJ; Edward Schillebeeckx

BOARD OF DIRECTORS
President: Felix Wilfred
Vice Presidents: Thierry-Marie Courau; Diego Irarrázaval; Susan Ross

BOARD OF EDITORS
Regina Ammicht Quinn (Frankfurt, Germany)
Mile Babić (Sarajevo, Bosnia-Herzogovina)
Maria Clara Bingemer (Rio de Janeiro, Brazil)
Erik Borgman (Nijmegen, The Netherlands)
Lisa Sowle Cahill (Boston, USA)
Frère Thierry-Marie Courau (Paris, France)
Hille Haker (Chicago, USA)
Diego Irarrázaval (Santiago, Chile)
Solange Lefebvre (Montreal, Canada)
Sarojini Nadar (Durban, South Africa)
Daniel Franklin Pilario (Quezon City, Philippines)
Susan Ross (Chicago, USA)
Silvia Scatena (Reggio Emilia, Italy)
Jon Sobrino SJ (San Salvador, El Salvador)
Luiz Carlos Susin (Porto Alegre, Brazil)
Andreś Torres Queiruga (Santiago de Compostela, Spain)
João J. Vila-Chã (Portugal)
Marie-Theres Wacker (Münster, Germany)
Felix Wilfred (Madras, India)

PUBLISHERS
SCM Press (London, UK)
Matthias-Grünewald Verlag (Ostfildern, Germany)
Editrice Queriniana (Brescia, Italy)
Editorial Verbo Divino (Estella, Spain)
EditoraVozes (Petropolis, Brazil)
Ex Libris and Synopsis (Rijeka, Croatia)

Concilium Secretariat:
Asian Centre for Cross-Cultural Studies,
40/6A, Panayur Kuppam Road, Sholinganallur Post, Panayur, Madras 600119, India.
Phone: +91- 44 24530682 Fax: +91- 44 24530443
E-mail: Concilium.madras@gmail.com
Managing Secretary: Arokia Mary Anthonidas

Concilium Subscription Information

February	**2015/1:** *Religion and Identity in Post-Conflict Societies*
April	**2015/2:** *Young Catholics Reshaping the Church*
July	**2015/3:** *Globalization and the Church of the Poor*
October	**2015/4:** *Theology, Anthropology and Neuroscience*
December	**2015/5:** *Silence*

New subscribers: to receive *Concilium 2015* (five issues) anywhere in the world, please copy this form, complete it in block capitals and send it with your payment to the address below.

Please enter my subscription for *Concilium 2015*

Individuals
____ £50 UK
____ £72 overseas and Eire
____ $95 North America/Rest of World
____ €85 Europe

Institutions
____ £72 UK
____ £92 overseas and Eire
____ $110 North America/Rest of World
____ €135 Europe

Postage included – airmail for overseas subscribers

Payment Details:
Payment must accompany all orders and can be made by cheque or credit card
I enclose a cheque for £/$/€_____ Payable to Hymns Ancient and Modern Ltd
Please charge my Visa/MasterCard (Delete as appropriate) for £/$/€ _____

Credit card number _____

Expiry date _____

Signature of cardholder_____

Name on card _____

Telephone _____E-mail _____

Send your order to *Concilium*, Hymns Ancient and Modern Ltd
13a Hellesdon Park Road, Norwich NR6 5DR, UK
E-mail: concilium@hymnsam.co.uk
or order online at www.conciliumjournal.co.uk

Customer service information
All orders must be prepaid. Subscriptions are entered on an annual basis (i.e. January to December). No refunds on subscriptions will be made after the first issue of the Journal has been despatched. If you have any queries or require information about other payment methods, please contact our Customer Services department.